Bead & Wire Jewelry Exposed

Margot Potter

Katie Hacker

Fernando DaSilva

NORTH LIGHT BOOKS
Cincinnati, Ohio
www.mycraftivity.com

Bead & Wire Jewelry Exposed. Copyright © 2008 by Margot Potter, Katie Hacker and Fernando DaSilva. Manufactured in China. All rights reserved. The written instructions, photographs, designs, patterns and projects in this volume are intended for the personal use of the reader and may be reproduced for that purpose only. Any other use, especially commercial use, is forbidden under law without the express written permission of the copyright holder. Violators will be prosecuted to the fullest extent of the law. No other part of this book may be reproduced in any form or by any electronic or mechanical means including information storage and retrieval systems without permission in writing from the publisher, except by a reviewer, who may quote a brief passage in review. Published by North Light Books, an imprint of F+W Publications, 4700 East Galbraith Road, Cincinnati, Ohio 45236. (800) 289-0963. First edition.

12 11 10   5 4 3

Distributed in Canada by Fraser Direct
100 Armstrong Avenue
Georgetown, ON, Canada L7G 5S4
Tel: (905) 877-4411

Distributed in the U.K. and Europe by David & Charles
Brunel House, Newton Abbot, Devon, TQ12 4PU, England
Tel: (+44) 1626 323200, Fax: (+44) 1626 323319
E-mail: postmaster@davidandcharles.co.uk

Distributed in Australia by Capricorn Link
P.O. Box 704, S. Windsor, NSW 2756 Australia
Tel: (02) 4577-3555

Library of Congress Cataloging-in-Publication Data

DaSilva, Fernando.
  Bead and wire jewelry exposed / Fernando DaSilva, Katie Hacker & Margot Potter. -- 1st ed.
     p. cm.
  Includes index.
  ISBN 978-1-60061-159-9 (pbk. : alk. paper)
 1. Jewelry making. 2. Beadwork. 3. Wire jewelry. I. Hacker, Katie. II. Potter, Margot. III. Title.
  TT212.D36 2008
  739.27'2--dc22
                                        2008026972

Editor: Jessica Gordon
Designer: Kelly O'Dell
Layout Designer: Steven Peters
Production Coordinator: Greg Nock
Photographers: Ric Deliantoni and Christine Polomsky
Stylist: Jan Nickum

F+W PUBLICATIONS, INC.

www.fwpublications.com

About the Authors

Fernando DaSilva

Fernando DaSilva was born and raised in Brazilia, the capital of exuberant Brazil. The modern architecture and the vivid colors and rhythms of Brazil, along with worldwide pop culture, are Fernando's biggest design influences. The result is dramatic jewelry with international flair, brilliant color and alluring texture. His work has appeared in many beading magazines and in *Women's Wear Daily*, where he was noted as a designer to watch. Fernando has created collections for Touchstone Crystal and he also has his own jewelry line, on display at www. dasilvajewelry.com. He says, "I like to work with simple jewelry techniques but I want to take my designs beyond the obvious."

Metric Conversion Chart

to convert	to	multiply by
Inches	Centimeters	2.54
Centimeters	Inches	0.4
Feet	Centimeters	30.5
Centimeters	Feet	0.03
Yards	Meters	0.9
Meters	Yards	1.1
Sq. Inches	Sq. Centimeters	6.45
Sq. Centimeters	Sq. Inches	0.16
Sq. Feet	Sq. Meters	0.09
Sq. Meters	Sq. Feet	10.8
Sq. Yards	Sq. Meters	0.8
Sq. Meters	Sq. Yards	1.2
Pounds	Kilograms	0.45
Kilograms	Pounds	2.2
Ounces	Grams	28.3
Grams	Ounces	0.035

Katie Hacker

Katie Hacker presents "Beading Lessons" on each episode of the public television series *Beads, Baubles & Jewels*, and draws in viewers with her approachable style and innovative techniques. Katie specializes in fashionable jewelry you can make tonight and wear tomorrow. She has written numerous books about beading and crafts, which have sold more than half a million copies. She contributes beading projects to a variety of publications and teaches workshops at national venues such as the Bead & Button Show and Bead Fest. Read Katie's blog and sign up for her monthly newsletter at www.katiehacker.com.

Margot Potter

Margot Potter is an internationally recognized designer, author, freelance writer, video personality, TV spokesperson, teacher, public speaker and consultant. Her designs reflect her uniquely eclectic view of the world at large and are a refreshing change of pace from the status quo. She is the author of the popular *The Impatient Beader* how-to jewelry-making series for North Light Books. She is also the author of *Beyond the Bead*. You can explore Margot's designs, The Impatient Crafter videos and her wildly popular daily blog at www.margotpotter.com.

Acknowledgments

The authors wish to thank Beadalon and Swarovski for providing the materials for this book. Mike Shields, Wyatt White, Yvette Rodriguez, Rebecca Whittaker and Nicole Harper have our extra-special thanks. Gratitude to the whole North Light team for their dedication to making this book a success, with special thanks to editor Jessica Gordon, photographer Christine Polomsky, book designer Kelly O'Dell, photo stylist Jan Nickum, and editorial director Christine Doyle. Fernando would also like to thank Bruno Cardoso, Jan Christy, Patty Aitson and Madame Ludeau for their support. He dedicates this book to his mother and Wyatt White. Katie thanks the Hackers, the Browns, and the crew of *Beads, Baubles & Jewels*. She dedicates this book to Craig and Lily since they are her favorite part of the day. Margot thanks her wonderful family, friends and devoted blog readers. She dedicates this book to Drew and Avalon because without them, there wouldn't be any sparkle at all.

Contents

Expose Your Creativity

Get ready to embark on an exciting adventure through the world of jewelry design. For the projects in this book, we've shifted the focus away from the obvious to highlight and expose design elements that are usually hidden. It's a new approach to jewelry making that we've developed through our work as the Beadalon Design Team and as teachers at the CREATE YOUR STYLE with CRYSTALLIZED – *Swarovski Elements* Tucson Event. We're thrilled to share our newly discovered techniques with you!

Inside *Bead & Wire Jewelry Exposed*, you'll see things you've never encountered before, including fabulous new materials and techniques that look intricate but are easy to create. You'll learn how to expose beading wire, chain and other components in completely unexpected ways, opening up a new realm of possibilities for incorporating unusual elements into jewelry designs and using traditional materials in innovative ways.

All of our projects feature Beadalon products and CRYSTALLIZED – *Swarovski Elements*. The materials we've used in this book are widely available in bead shops, craft stores and online, but they are easy to customize for your own purposes. When substituting beads from your stash, keep in mind that overall size is the most important factor to match. Change the stringing material's diameter if necessary to accommodate the bead's hole size.

What is it that makes these designs so intriguing? Is it the unexpected use of findings and other supporting elements as focal pieces? Is it the clean lines and striking simplicity? Is it the dramatic use of color? That's for you to decide. We're exposing the design secrets and showing you the tricks of the trade. Now it's up to you to take these tools and create designs that suit you.

Seize the bead!

Margot, Katie & Fernando

Materials

Findings

Findings are the mechanical parts of jewelry making—they're the fasteners and components a jewelry maker uses to assemble jewelry. Such items include clasps, connectors, bead caps, eye pins, head pins, spacers and crimps, among many others. In addition to using standard findings, the projects in this book use some of the newest and most clever findings available, including Wire Guardians, EZ-Crimp ends, Scrimp findings and Bead Bumpers miniature stretch beads.

Clasps

A clasp is any kind of closure used to secure a necklace or bracelet. Some of the most popular clasps include lobster, toggle, magnetic and S-hook clasps.

Lobster clasps provide a very secure connection. A small lever opens and closes to link to the other end of the jewelry piece.

Toggle clasps consist of an open "O" ring and a toggle bar. One half is attached to each end of the piece of jewelry, and the toggle fits through the O ring to fasten it. Toggles are especially nice for heavier designs and for bracelets. The end of the design must be small enough to fit through the ring part of the toggle.

Magnetic clasps come in a variety of shapes. They're strong and eliminate fumbling with tiny latches and hooks.

S-hook clasps consist of two S-shaped hooks that create a symmetrical look. Close one hook and leave the other slightly open for easy fastening. S-hooks are perfect to use with multistrand necklaces.

Ear Wires

Earrings findings come in various styles. Attach beaded dangles to an earring finding to make quick jewelry.

Lever-back earring wires provide a secure hold without the need for additional findings. The formed wires are round and comfortable to wear.

Hoops are a quick and easy way to create earrings. Simply slide on beads, charms and dangles, using Bead Bumpers as stoppers.

General Findings

These general findings are the workhorses of jewelry making. You'll use them to finish pieces, to create dangles and to link components. Here is a list of the findings we most commonly use.

EZ-Crimp ends allow you to attach crimps directly to flexible stringing wire. Once your design is secured with an EZ-Crimp end, it can be attached to any clasp according to your preference. EZ-Crimp ends are available in sterling silver and plated metal. There are even EZ-Crimp clasps available in toggle, S-hook and hook-and-eye versions. Simply crimp the clasp to either end of the jewelry piece for an all-in-one solution.

Bead Bumpers are miniature stretch beads that look like a knot when placed between beads on stringing wire. They are available in oval and cube shapes, and in a variety of colors.

Eyeglass holders are adjustable links made of black rubber or clear silicon that may be used as connectors.

Crimp beads and tubes are the most popular findings for securing clasps to jewelry, or for stationing beads on wire. Crimp beads and tubes may also be used as accent or spacer beads.

Scrimp findings are the newest method for securing beaded strands. A little screw inside each Scrimp holds stringing wire in place. The finding is removable and reusable. Available in bullet, oval and round shapes, these findings are strong and stylish.

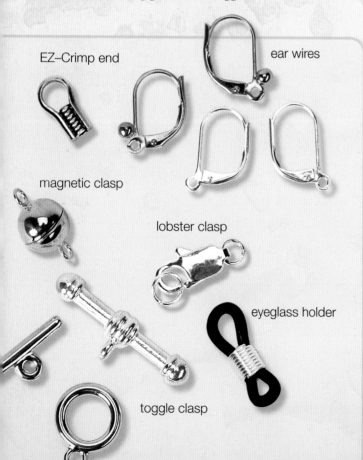

EZ–Crimp end

ear wires

magnetic clasp

lobster clasp

eyeglass holder

toggle clasp

Wire Guardian findings are rigid pieces that protect stringing wire from abrasion. Wire is threaded through the guardian, then crimped in place, minimizing tension.

Pinch bails take the stress out of wire wrapping briolettes. Simply squeeze or pinch the outer portion of the finding until the pointed end begins to enter the holes of the bead or pendant. Pinch bails can also be used to link donut-style stones or round beads.

Head and **eye pins** are used to create dangles, charms or clusters of beads. Head pins resemble thin nails and eye pins have a loop on one end. Eye pins can be used to link beads, or they can be threaded through a cone to conceal multiple wires linked to the eye pin's loop.

Jump rings come in a variety of sizes and gauges and are used to link elements together.

Cones are usually made of metal and are great for making earrings, necklaces and bracelets. The starting and ending points for multistrand designs can be easily hidden inside a cone.

Bead caps are decorative findings that are less than half the size of a bead. They offer color, texture and a lacy look to your beaded creations.

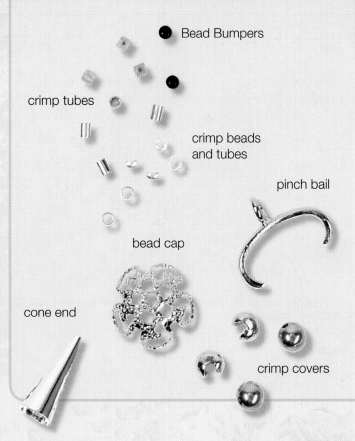

Bead Bumpers

crimp tubes

crimp beads and tubes

pinch bail

bead cap

cone end

crimp covers

Solid rings are heavy-duty closed rings made of sheet metal. They're great to use when a sturdy connection is necessary. Slide a solid ring onto a rubber cord, link it to a chain with jump rings, or wire wrap it in place.

Metal connectors have multiple holes and are perfect for building long, structured necklaces or earrings.

Crimp covers are open, round metal beads that slide over crimped beads or tubes to conceal them. They add a refined finish.

Memory wire end caps are open on one side to accommodate memory wire. Some versions come with a ring at the end for adding a bead or charm dangle.

Cord ends have small teeth that "bite" onto a suede or faux suede cord when flattened. Attach a clasp to the loop on the cord end.

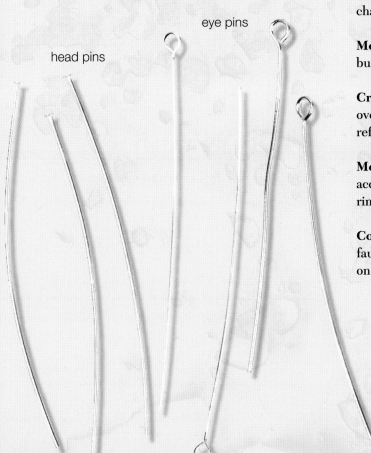

eye pins

head pins

9

Chain and Stringing Materials

Most jewelry pieces are built using a base of chain or stringing material. In this book, we use a wide range of chain and wire. Understanding the differences of both is important, as each has a different look and durability. Use the following information to understand your choices as you begin to create your own jewelry.

Chain

A series of links connected together is called chain. It can be made of metal, Lucite, acrylic, plastic, polyester or wood. Chain comes in a wide variety of styles, including cabled, elongated, rolo, double-ball, diamond-shaped and chain maille.

Quick Link components are individual solid links that can be linked together to create a simple chain as well as to create entire linked sections. Quick Links come in assorted geometric shapes.

Polyester chain is made of polyester fibers fashioned into a large cable chain. Use polyester chain in place of traditional chain to add a dash of color. It's also great for big and bold earring designs without excess weight.

Plated metal chain is available in a variety of styles and finishes. The projects in this book use unsoldered chain, which makes it possible to connect the chain directly to a variety of findings without a jump ring or other connector.

Stringing Materials

Stringing materials range from wire and thread to leather strands and stretchy elastic. For most of the stringing projects in this book, we've used different types of Beadalon stringing wire. For the last thirty years, Beadalon has been the originator, innovator and manufacturer of bead-stringing wire. Their wire is unique in the industry because Beadalon is the only company that makes its own wire, strand and cable for bead stringing.

The manufacturing difference allows Beadalon to design and produce exciting new wire products in-house, such as the industry's first silver-plated and 24K gold-plated wires. Beadalon also produces a wide selection of wire flexibilities, diameters, colors and spool lengths.

Beadalon beading wire is made from stranded threads of miniature stainless steel wire, making it as strong as steel but as soft as thread. The number of miniature wires determines its flexibility. Choose the diameter that works best with the bead hole size, unless a different wire is specified in the instructions. In addition to the standard colors—bright, black and bronze—Beadalon beading wire

is available in a wide variety of colors and metallic finishes. It is best for stringing projects featuring glass, crystal, metal and semiprecious beads.

Plated colored wire combines the flexibility and strength of stainless steel wire with the luster of precious metal. This is a great alternative for jewelry designers who want the quality of fine silver or 24K gold but need the additional strength and durability of stainless steel.

Colourcraft wire

silk thread

rubber tubing

faux suede cord

Greek leather

memory wire

plated beading wire

plated metal chain

Quick Links components

polyester chain

Metallic beading wire mimics the look of precious metal. It has a slightly lower breaking strength than other beading wire in the same diameter and construction.

.925 sterling silver beading wire is made of miniature strands of solid sterling silver wires twisted together. A thin, clear layer of nylon covers it to prolong strand life and prevent kinking. It adds an extra level of quality for the beading purist. This wire is best for lightweight, precious beaded jewelry.

Satin wire has a soft, silky feel and a unique matte finish. The satin colors of silver, gold and copper provide a lovely contrast to sparkly crystal beads and offer a nice alternative to regular beading wire.

Clear color wire is stainless steel wire coated in nylon. The wire is available in a variety of rainbow hues. The nylon coating allows light to pass through and reflect off the bright stainless steel wire. That spark of color makes beaded designs come alive!

Crinkle Wire bead stringing wire is permanently wavy wire that can be used to add texture to beaded designs. It has the same flexibility and breaking strength as regular 7-strand beading wire.

Colourcraft wire is permanently colored copper wire typically used for wire wrapping. This special shaping wire is available in a variety colors and diameters, which are referred to by gauge. As the gauge number gets smaller, the wire diameter gets thicker. For example, 20-gauge is thicker than 28-gauge.

German-style plated wire is an economical alternative to sterling silver or gold-filled wire. It is typically used for wire wrapping and is available in a variety of diameters.

Memory wire is tempered wire that retains its coiled form. It's available in preformed necklace, bracelet and ring sizes. No clasp is necessary because memory wire automatically stays in place on your neck, wrist or fingers. Only use shears specially made to cut hardened wire—memory wire will ruin ordinary wire cutters.

Silk thread and **cord** come in a variety of colors and diameters. Choose the diameter that works best with the bead hole size. It is typically sold on a card with a needle attached. Stretch any creases out before knotting. Silk cord is traditionally used to string pearls and other gemstones with a knot between each bead. Poly-nylon cord is a less expensive, synthetic alternative to silk. It has less stretch but is also available in a variety of colors and sizes.

Elasticity cord is a single-strand stretchy beading cord available in a variety of colors, including clear, black, pink, green, blue and purple. It's the perfect choice for making quick, inexpensive stretchy bracelets. Elasticity is available in .5mm, .8mm and 1mm. Choose the diameter of the cord based on the bead hole size. The cord should pass comfortably through the bead holes.

Rubber tubing is hollow cord that can be used by itself or in combination with other stringing materials. It's available in different diameters, colors and finishes, including a velour version. Rubber tubing is commonly used to cover memory wire or beading wire.

Faux suede cord is softer than genuine suede and tends to lay flatter when used in a beaded design. It's available in an array of colors and can be knotted or used with cord ends.

Greek leather is round leather cord with a very soft, supple texture. It's available in a variety of colors and widths. Use it with round cord ends for a finished look.

Beads and Pendants

There is a reason the top haute couture houses turn to CRYSTALLIZED – *Swarovski Elements* when they want to dazzle their audiences—it is without question the finest cut crystal on the planet. CRYSTALLIZED – *Swarovski Elements* are mechanically precision cut to exacting standards to create smooth through holes that are easy on wire and other stringing materials. They are available in a mind-boggling variety of shapes, sizes and colors that will endlessly spark the designer's imagination. No other beading material has the same sparkle, beauty and cache.

Rounds

CRYSTALLIZED basic round beads come in a wide variety of colors and sizes, making them a go-to bead for virtually any project. (Not every bead comes in every color, but there are so many choices that you should have no problem finding the right bead for your designs.) The 2mm beads are so small and uniform you can use them for weaving applications. The 20mm size beads make fabulous focal beads in bold and striking designs. Use rounds as spacer beads or for multistrand vintage looks or as the basic building block for any idea. In addition to this particular style of round bead, there are many other styles and colors with a variety of faceting.

Bicones

Bicones offer the widest variety of colors, finishes and sizes of any style bead in their catalog. Bicones are fabulous no matter how you use them. They give a different dimension to woven pieces and work great as spacer beads in strung designs. They come in sizes ranging from 3mm to 12mm, with each individual size creating an entirely different vibe. Try mixing colors and sizes to create exciting new effects. Bicones also come in a top-drilled style. Hang these from a wire or bunch them together between larger beads or metal components.

Teardrops, Briolettes and Rondelles

These shapes give designers more bead weaponry for their arsenals. The teardrop bead is simply faceted and has a top-to-bottom through hole, which makes it ideal for making earrings or for creating drops to incorporate into necklaces or bracelets. The briolette bead is top-drilled, so it can hang down on a strung design or be threaded onto a jump ring to create a dangle. The rondelle is a fabulous spacer bead and adds a different dimension to your work. All three of these beads are available in a wide variety of colors, shapes and sizes. In addition, CRYSTALLIZED – *Swarovski Elements*

makes other beads with similar shapes and varied facets in limited colors.

Special Shapes, Pendants and Filigrees

Pendants, beads and crystal components in special shapes are great fun to integrate into your work. Open circles and squares inspire endless design ideas. Cubes drilled from top to bottom and diagonally are an interesting geometric option. Stars, hearts, crosses and moons provide a touch of whimsy or make a bold statement. The new twist stone comes in a bead and a sew-on shape, and it is faceted differently on the front and back, making it a versatile addition to your beadwork. Each season, CRYSTALLIZED – *Swarovski Elements* creates new shapes such as the cubist bead, polygon, starfish pendant, cosmic shape, avant garde and helix bead. Their metal filigree beads and components are stunning, too, and give your work a whole new dimension. Be on the lookout for their latest innovations— they are always inspired and inspiring!

special shapes, pendants and filigrees

teardrops, briolettes and rondelles

rounds

bicones

Tools

Quality tools are a necessity for creating quality designs: Nothing will frustrate you more than working with poor-quality tools and materials. We've broken down the tools used to make the projects in this book so you can carefully consider what you need. The most important tools you need to get started are round-nose pliers, chain-nose pliers, crimping pliers and wire cutters. Once you've mastered the jewelry basics, you will find yourself hungry to explore new tools and techniques. This guide will be a great reference for you as you expand your repertoire.

Round-nose pliers have tapered, round jaws used to curve and loop wire. They are an essential tool for creating links for bracelets, necklaces and earrings. They're a must-have for wire-wrapping designs.

Chain-nose pliers are the jewelry version of needle-nose pliers. Use them to bend wire at right angles and to open and close wire loops and jump rings. They're also great for grabbing the Sbeady wire needle when threading beading wire through hollow rubber tubing.

Wire cutters are essential for jewelry makers. There are several kinds of cutters. Flush cutters have a flush side that allows for a crisp, sharp cut. They can be used on most soft wires, such as Colourcraft wire, Beadalon stringing wire and other soft wires up to 16-gauge. Use cutters with small tips to ensure a smooth, close cut. Keep different cutters for base metal and precious metals.

Memory wire shears are designed specifically for cutting hard wire, such as memory wire. Memory wire compromises the blades of ordinary wire cutters. Shears leave a clean, safe-to-handle straight edge on memory wire and can also be used to cut jewelry cable.

Crimp tools are used to close crimp tubes and beads around the wire without compromising their strength and durability. Using a crimp tool properly gives your creation a professional look. There are three different sizes of crimp tools. Use the micro-crimp tool with #1 crimp tubes and #0 crimp beads; use the standard crimp tool with #1–2 crimp beads and #2 crimp tubes; and use the mighty-crimp tool with #3–4 crimp tubes and #3 crimp beads. All Beadalon wire spools are marked with the correct sizes of crimp beads and tubes to be used with that wire.

EZ-Crimp pliers are designed exclusively to fit EZ-Crimp ends and clasps. Simply place the EZ-Crimp end into the jaw of the EZ-Crimp pliers with the smooth part in the curved tip of the jaw. Squeeze until the coil section is completely tight, securing the connection with the wire.

The **Beadalon knotter** was created to make tight, consistent, professional-looking knotted strands of beads. They can be used with pearls, crystals, gemstones and any other bead. Once you've perfected this technique, the knotter allows for rapid knotting and re-stringing.

A **Beadalon wire twister** is used to make tight and consistent twisted wire lengths. Place up to five wires into the disc, and then attach the twister to a sturdy object; pull the wires taut, turn the crank and watch the wires twist. Try twisting wires in multiple colors together to create multicolor jump rings for extra pizzazz.

A **Beadalon jump ring maker** creates any size jump ring needed for your designs. Choose the correct size mandrel, attach it to the handle, insert the wire and wrap the wire around the mandrel. Once you've wrapped the wire as many times as desired, use flush cutters to cut three to four wraps at a time, reversing the cutter after the first cut and making an additional flush cut, leaving two flat ends on each jump ring.

The **Beadalon spiral maker** is a handy wire tool that creates perfect reproducible spirals out of Colourcraft, German-style and any other soft wire. Use the diameter wire needed for the spiral as washers on each of the screws (this keeps the two acrylic parts the necessary distance apart so the wire will coil correctly). Insert the "T" into the acrylic holder and feed the end of the wire to be coiled into the slit. Turn the "T" until the desired diameter of spiral is made. Pull the "T" out of the base

and the spiral should slip out. If the spiral is stuck, loosen the screws slightly to free it.

A **Beadalon bead opener tool** is used to open and close crimp covers. The long, pointed part of the tool is called an awl. Just place a seamed bead onto the awl and press down into the acrylic block to open the bead. Repeat this step on the other side of the bead to open it fully. Place the opened C-shaped bead over the crimp and use EZ-Crimp pliers or the mighty-crimp tool to close the opened bead and hide the crimp.

A **battery-operated bead reamer** enlarges the holes in pearls, gemstones or other beads, and it can be used to enlarge the holes in an EZ-Crimp end as well. To use the reamer, submerge the tip in a small bowl of water, press the button and ream the hole from both sides of the bead. This is a real time-saver tool!

A **Sbeady wire needle** is a sharp needle with an easy-slide half-open portion for slipping the stringing wire into the hollow section. This needle can pierce velour and rubber tubing.

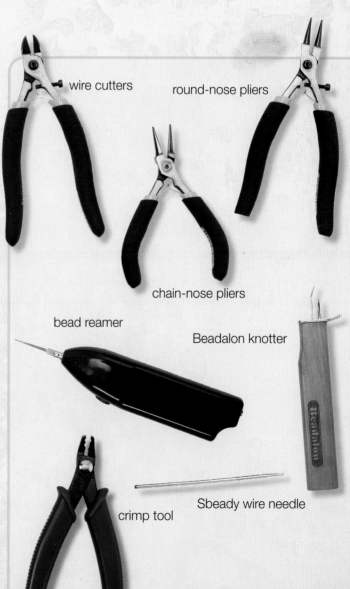

wire cutters

round-nose pliers

chain-nose pliers

bead reamer

Beadalon knotter

crimp tool

Sbeady wire needle

1
Technicolor Dreams
Designs Featuring Colored Wire

Combining colored wire and crystals adds a whole new dimension to beaded jewelry designs. It's interesting how a subtle change, such as swapping out plain wire for the colored variety, often has such a big impact. Suddenly, something sedate becomes outrageous, or a day-to-day idea is elevated to extraordinary. Experiment with different combinations of colored wire and beads—the color play that results with each new combination is fascinating. This colorful Beadalon wire is far too pretty to hide, and it's a perfect fit for the wonderful color palette available from CRYSTALLIZED – *Swarovski Elements*. Why be a wallflower when you can bloom like an orchid?

You'll be red hot and saucy in the *Fire & Spice* necklace (see page 18). Or try the design in a cool color combo for a waterfall effect. Wish upon a star and look like one at the same time in the *Night Sky* necklace (see page 26). What if you did this in bright colors or cool tones? The *Fireworks* necklace (see page 23) is the perfect combination of sophistication and modern edge—it offers an innovative new technique for using colored wire.

By Katie Hacker

Rosy Illusions

Illusion necklaces are ever popular, and it's no wonder since they look great with many different necklines. The design challenge is keeping them fresh and contemporary looking. One way to update the style is by choosing beads in trendy colors and shapes. In this monochromatic rose version, I've mixed funky helix crystals with traditional rounds and bicones. Multiple strands give it extra eye-catching appeal.

Materials

12 8mm rose water opal round crystal beads

6 8mm light rose helix crystal beads

31 6mm light rose helix crystal beads

14 6mm rose water opal round crystal beads

12 6mm rose alabaster bicone crystal beads

.018" (.45mm) pink 19-strand beading wire

36 6mm silver round beaded solid rings

3-strand EZ-Crimp sterling silver toggle clasp

78 #1 silver crimp tubes

Tools

mighty-crimp tool or EZ-Crimp pliers

chain-nose pliers

wire cutters

16

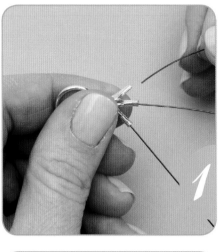

ONE • Crimp wire ends

Cut strands of beading wire to the following lengths: 16" (41cm), 17" (43cm) and 18" (46cm). Place 1 end of the shortest wire inside an EZ-Crimp end and use a mighty-crimp tool to squeeze the sides together. Attach an EZ-Crimp end to 1 end of the 17" (43cm) and 18" (46cm) wires as well. (See Techniques, page 139, for instructions on securing wire with an EZ-Crimp end.)

TWO • Crimp first bead station in place

Slide a crimp tube onto the shortest wire. Use chain-nose pliers to flatten the crimp 2" (5cm) from the EZ-Crimp end. String a 6mm rose water opal bead and another crimp tube onto the wire. Flatten the crimp tube with chain-nose pliers to secure the bead.

THREE • Finish beading first wire

Leave ½" (1cm) and attach a crimp tube, then string on a 6mm helix, ring, 8mm rose water opal, ring, 6mm helix and crimp tube. Flatten the tube to secure the beaded station. String on 9 more beaded stations, alternating between a 1-bead station and a 3-bead station, and leaving ½" (1cm) between each station.

FOUR • Begin beading second wire

Slide a crimp tube, a 6mm helix bead and a crimp tube onto the 17" (43cm) wire, and secure the beaded station 1½" (4cm) from the EZ-Crimp end.

FIVE • Finish beading necklace

Leave ½" (2cm) and secure the next beaded station between 2 crimp tubes: rose alabaster, ring, 8mm helix, ring, rose alabaster. String on 11 more beaded stations, alternating between a 1-bead station and the 3-bead station, and leaving ½" (2cm) between each station. Bead the longest wire, alternating between the same 2 stations as for the first strand, beginning 1" (3cm) from the EZ-Crimp end and leaving ½" (2cm) between beaded stations.

SIX • Finish necklace

Secure the free ends of the wires to the remaining multistrand EZ-Crimp toggle clasp component in the same manner as in step 1.

tip

To plan your own illusion design, arrange all of the beads on a bead board before stringing them. Laying the beads out allows you to see what the design will look like and ensures the beaded units are spaced evenly along the beading wire.

By Margot Potter

Fire & Spice

Oh, how fun is this fiery bib necklace? The wire tendrils look like flaming vines cascading from a simple woven-core necklace. The color combination was the result of playing around with several ideas until this one pulled everything together thematically. Now this is hot.

Materials

32 8mm top-drilled black diamond crystal bicones

22 6mm hyacinth crystal bicones

53 4mm fire opal crystal bicones

.018" (.45mm) 7-strand Beadalon red beading wire

5mm silver-plated jump ring

silver-plated lobster clasp

15 #2 silver-plated crimp tubes

Tools

mighty-crimp tool

chain-nose pliers

wire cutters

bead board or mat (optional)

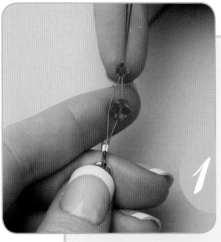

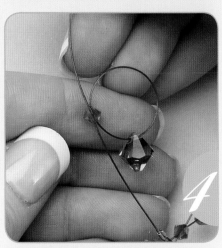

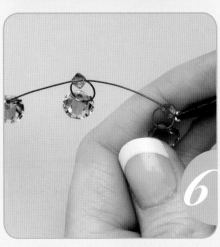

ONE • Begin to bead core strand

Cut a 40" (102cm) length of red wire and fold it in half. Slide a jump ring onto the wire so it rests in the fold. Slide a crimp tube onto both wires about ⅛" (3mm) from the jump ring. Flatten the crimp tube with a crimp tool. (See Techniques, page 138, for instructions on securing wire with a crimp tube.) Slide a hyacinth crystal onto 1 wire. Slide a fire opal crystal onto both wires.

TWO • Finish beading core strand

Slide a hyacinth crystal onto the opposite wire from the first and slide a fire opal crystal onto both wires. Continue stringing beads in this pattern, alternating sides as you work. Adjust the wires to create tension, but not so much that the design becomes stiff or warped. After stringing the final hyacinth bead, secure the lobster clasp to the wire with a crimp tube, using chain-nose pliers to pull the wires through the crimp tube, leaving approximately a 1⁄16" (2mm) loop above the top of the crimp tube to prevent wire wear. Trim the wires using wire cutters.

THREE • Attach wire for central tendril

Thread a crimp tube onto a 12" (31cm) section of red wire. Bring the end of the wire through the core strand at the center point of the necklace, looping the wire around the wire without the bead. Bring the wire end through the crimp tube to form a loop. Secure the loop by crimping the tube.

FOUR • Create loop

Thread a fire opal bicone and a black diamond bicone onto the wire, leaving approximately 1" (3cm) between the crimp tube and the first bead. Bring the wire back around itself and into the top of the fire opal crystal, forming a loop. Tighten the loop so the black diamond crystal dangles, but not so taut it's stiff.

FIVE • Finish beading central tendril

Move down the wire about 1" (3cm) and repeat the process. Create a total of 6 looped dangles. Thread the wire end into a crimp tube and use a pair of chain-nose pliers to flatten the tube. Make sure the tube is completely secured. Cut off the excess wire.

SIX • Create remaining tendrils

Move over to the next set of open wires and attach a 10" (25cm) section of wire to the wire without a bead on the outside of the bead above. Bead as before, creating 5 looped dangles and finishing with a crimp tube. Repeat for the opposite side. Move down again, repeating the process with 2 8" (20cm) strands with 4 looped dangles. Move down 1 last time, repeating with 2 8" (20cm) strands and 4 looped dangles.

By Margot Potter

Cool Down

Several years ago, I figured out how to weave
two wires in and out of single beads, stationing
them so they appeared to float on the wire as if
by magic. Honestly, it was because I was tired of
gluing and crimping beads in place and I needed
a faster method of stationing them. Since then
I have continued to experiment with different
configurations of wires and beads, including varying
sizes, shapes and number of beads. This design
features four wires woven in and out of four beads
of varied color and shape. The wire and beads are of
equal importance in this kind of design, so colored
wire is especially appealing.

Materials

9 14mm crystal twist beads

11 9mm x 6mm aqua
crystal teardrops

11 9mm x 6mm tanzanite
crystal teardrops

11 6mm olivine crystal bicones

.018" (.045mm) 7-strand blue
Beadalon wire

.018" (.045mm) 7-strand purple
Beadalon wire

2 5mm silver-plated jump rings

2 3mm silver-plated jump rings

1 sterling silver triangle toggle

3 sterling silver head pins

2 #4 crimp tubes

Tools

mighty-crimp pliers

round-nose pliers

2 pairs chain-nose pliers

wire cutters

bead mat or board (optional)

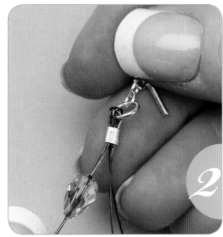

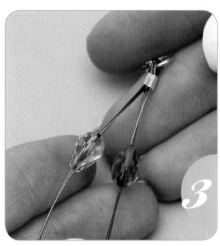

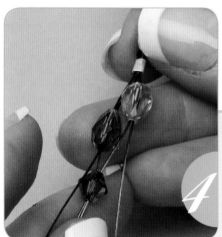

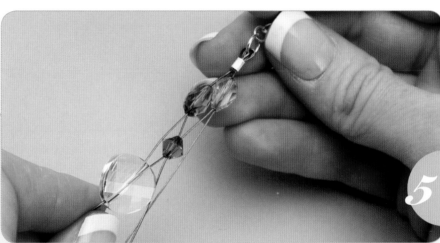

ONE • Crimp wires
Cut 2 30" (76cm) lengths of purple wire and 2 30" (76cm) lengths of blue wire. Secure all 4 wires to the second jump ring linked to a toggle bar with a crimp tube, using chain-nose pliers to pull the wires through the crimp tube, and leaving approximately a 1/16" (2mm) loop above the top of the crimp tube to prevent wire wear. (See Techniques, page 138, for instructions on securing wires with a crimp tube.) Trim the wire ends flush to the end of the crimp tube with wire cutters.

TWO • Thread on aqua teardrop
Thread an aqua teardrop onto 1 set of blue and purple wires.

THREE • Thread on tanzanite teardrop
Thread a tanzanite teardrop onto the remaining 2 wires.

FOUR • Thread on olivine bicone
Thread an olivine bicone onto the inner 2 wires.

FIVE • Thread on twist bead
Thread a twist bead onto the outer set of wires on the left side.

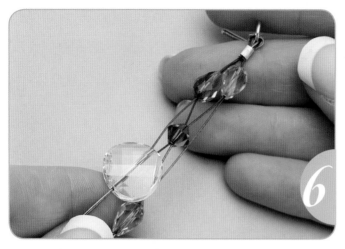

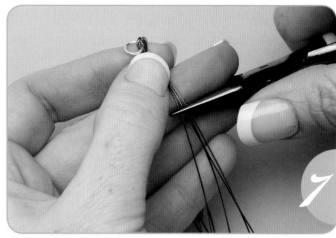

SIX • Thread on aqua teardrop

Thread an aqua teardrop bead onto the outer set of wires on the right side.

SEVEN • Finish stringing and adjust tension

Continue weaving the outer and inner wires into the beads in the established pattern in the following order: aqua teardrop, tanzanite teardrop, olivine bicone and twist bead. As you work, continuously adjust the tension, making sure the design is not too loose or too tight. It should drape somewhat, without having the beads move very much between the wires. When you reach the final olivine bicone, work back through the design a final time to adjust the tension. (Make sure there are 10 of each teardrop and olivine bead and 9 twist beads in the design.) Secure all the wires to a 5mm jump ring with a crimp tube, as in step 1. Trim the wires flush to the end of the crimp tube.

EIGHT • Attach triangle toggle component

Attach the toggle triangle to the right side of the design with a jump ring. (See Techniques, page 141, for instructions on opening and closing a jump ring.)

NINE • Add dangles

Create 3 coiled dangles using the sterling silver head pins: 1 with an olivine bead, 1 with an aqua bead and 1 with a tanzanite bead. Attach all 3 dangles to a 5mm jump ring, then link the dangles to the toggle triangle.

By Fernando DaSilva

Fireworks

Crystals suspended on rays of multicolored wire bring to mind a festive night highlighted by an explosion of pyrotechnics. This necklace combines the rich texture of velour tubing with the flash of colored stringing wire and dazzling crystals. When you wear this piece, you'll be the embodiment of casual glamour.

Tools

Sbeady wire needle

chain-nose pliers

Beadalon crimp cover tool

standard crimping pliers

wire cutters

Materials

2 8mm burgandy crystal rounds

2 8mm fuchsia crystal rounds

2 8mm purple velvet crystal rounds

3 8mm topaz AB crystal rounds

4 8mm crystal nut rounds

8 6mm crystal nut rounds

5 6mm burgandy crystal rounds

6 6mm golden shadow crystal rounds

8 4mm topaz crystal rounds

6 6mm burgandy crystal bicones

9 6mm fuchsia crystal bicones

7 6mm Indian red crystal bicones

9 6mm light Colorado topaz crystal bicones

7 6mm purple velvet crystal bicones

3 6mm topaz crystal bicones

7 4mm fuchsia crystal bicones

4 4mm Indian red crystal bicones

16 4mm light topaz crystal bicones

16" (41cm) brown velour tubing

40" (102cm) .018" (.45mm) 19-strand red clear colors Beadalon wire

30" (76cm) .018" (.45mm) 19-strand purple clear color Beadalon wire

30" (76cm) .018" (.45mm) 19-strand pink clear color Beadalon wire

1 stainless steel claw-end clasp

13 10mm gold-plated bead caps

130 #1 gold-plated crimp tubes

13 3.5mm gold-plated crimp covers

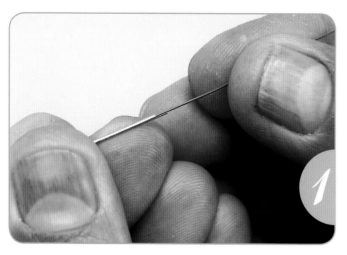

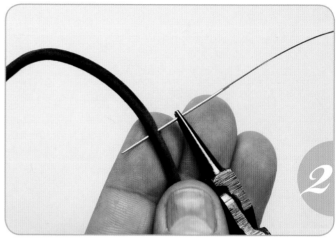

ONE • Prepare wire for threading

Cut 4 10" (25cm) lengths each of red, purple and pink wires. Set them aside. Slip a piece of red wire all the way into the end of the Sbeady wire needle using the open portion to guide the wire into the hole.

TWO • Thread red wire through tubing

Find the center of the velour tubing and puncture the tubing with the Sbeady wire needle. Use chain-nose pliers to pull the wire through the tube, leaving approximately 7½" (19cm) of wire below the tubing.

THREE • Bead first strand of wire

Slide a 4mm fuchsia bicone followed by a #1 crimp tube onto the wire protruding above the tubing. Use chain-nose pliers to flatten the crimp. Slide a bicone bead of your choice onto the wire protruding below the tubing and secure it in place by flattening a crimp tube below the bead with chain-nose pliers, leaving approximately ¼" (6mm) of wire between the crimp and the tubing. Repeat for a total of 6 bicones, leaving approximately ¼" (6mm) of wire between the beads.

FOUR • Finish beading first strand

Approximately ½" (2cm) down from the last bicone, string on a crimp tube, a bead cap, an 8mm round bead and a final crimp tube. Flatten both crimp tubes with chain-nose pliers, trapping the bead cap and round as snugly between them as possible. Trim away the excess wire below the final crimp tube flush with the bottom of the tube.

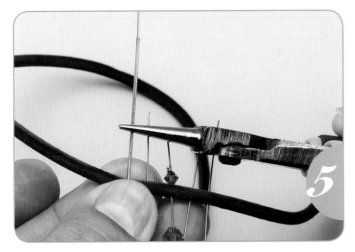

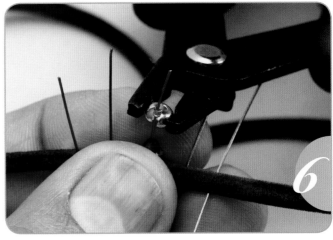

Do not be attached to perfection on this design—just "eyeball" the spaces between beads and choose color combinations based on what you like. If you are more of a silver girl, try making a clear version with white metal bead caps and crimp tubes. Play with crystal beads in ocean shades such as blue and green accentuated with a splash of citrus.

tip

FIVE • Bead remaining strands

Continue puncturing and securing wires as in steps 1–4, working out from the center on both sides. Alternate wire colors on each side of the central wire in the following sequence: purple, pink, red. Bead each wire with a random assortment of 3mm, 4mm and 6mm bicones and rounds. End each wire with the same bead cap and 8mm round bead pairing as in the center strand (as described in step 4). When piercing the velour tubing with the Sbeady wire needle, make certain the wires are perpendicular with the velour tubing. Continue beading wires until there is a total of 13 beaded wires.

SIX • Cover crimps

Cover each crimp tube at the top of each wire strand with a crimp cover. Slide the crimp cover over a crimp tube and then place the cover inside the first indention in the jaws of the crimp tool. Squeeze gently to cover the crimp. (See Techniques, page 138, for instructions on using a crimp cover.) Trim any wire ends flush to the bottom edge of the crimp covers.

SEVEN • Attach clasp to cord ends

Attach a stainless steel claw-end clasp to both sides of the velour tubing using crimping pliers to drive the claws into the tubing.

By Katie Hacker

Night Sky

Who isn't inspired by these gorgeous crystal moon and star charms? I wanted to make a piece that looked just as celestial as the components. Adding wire dangles turned out to be just the ticket. The black beading wire creates dangles that look delicate but bold at the same time, and they create a shooting star effect. Attaching extra wire at the ends allows you to braid the sides of the necklace without creating too much bulk to pass through the bead holes in the center of the design.

Materials

1 30mm crystal AB moon crystal pendant

4 20mm jet star crystal pendants

4 8mm crystal AB helix crystal beads

8 8mm jet/silver crystal rondelles

12 6mm crystal AB helix crystal beads

33 4mm jet helix crystal beads

.018" (.45mm) 19-strand black beading wire

4 6mm silver jump rings

sterling silver EZ-Crimp toggle clasp

5 #1 silver crimp beads

5 #3 silver crimp beads

12 #1 silver crimp tubes

Tools

standard crimping pliers

mighty-crimp tool or EZ-Crimp pliers

chain-nose pliers

wire cutters

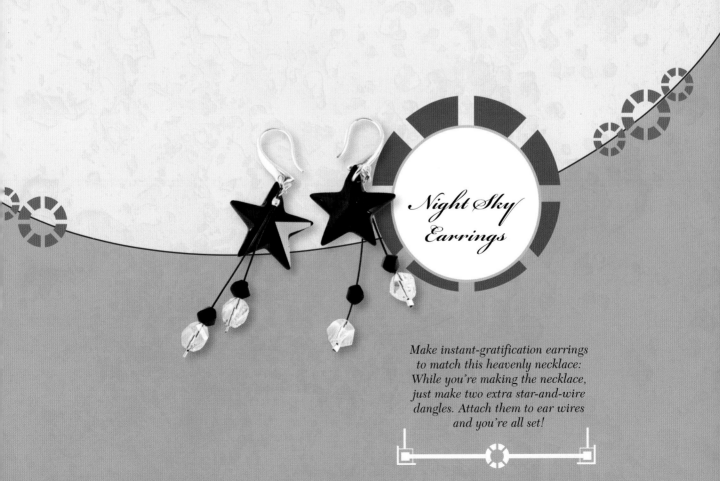

Night Sky Earrings

Make instant-gratification earrings to match this heavenly necklace: While you're making the necklace, just make two extra star-and-wire dangles. Attach them to ear wires and you're all set!

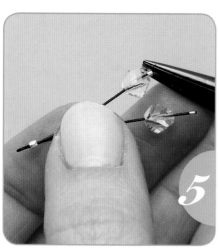

ONE • Begin to create central tassel

Cut strands of black beading wire to the following lengths: 1 17" (43cm) strand, 1 8" (20cm) strand, 5 6" (15cm) strands, and 5 3" (8cm) strands. Hold an 8" (20cm) and a 6" (15cm) piece of wire together and fold them in half. Pass the ends through a #3 crimp bead and slide it up close to the fold; use a mighty-crimp tool to crimp it. (See Techniques, page 138, for instructions on securing wire with a crimp tube.)

TWO • Add beads to tassel

String a 4mm jet crystal and a 6mm crystal AB bead onto each wire end. Place a #1 crimp tube on the end of each wire and use chain-nose pliers to gently flatten each crimp.

THREE • Begin to create beaded bail

String a #1 crimp bead, 5 4mm jet crystals, the moon pendant and the tassel from step 2 onto a 3" (8cm) piece of beading wire. Pass the wire end through the crimp bead to form a beaded circle.

FOUR • Finish beaded bail

Tighten the circle, making sure the crimp bead is behind the moon pendant. Use chain-nose pliers to flatten the crimp.

FIVE • Make small tassels

Fold a 3" (8cm) piece of beading wire in half and pass both ends through a #1 crimp bead. Use standard crimping pliers to crimp the bead. String a 6mm crystal AB bead onto each wire end and secure them with #1 crimp tubes.

SIX • Finish star tassles

Link a star charm to the small dangle with a jump ring. (See Techniques, page 141, for instructions on opening and closing a jump ring.) Repeat steps 5–6 to make a total of 4 star tassels.

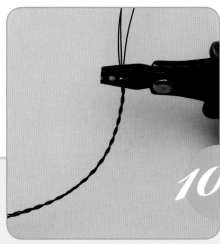

SEVEN • String center sequence of necklace

String the moon pendant onto the center of the 17" (43cm) piece of beading wire. String the following beads onto each side of the moon pendant: 6mm crystal AB, rondelle, 8mm crystal AB, rondelle, 6mm crystal AB.

EIGHT • Finish stringing necklace

On each side of the necklace, string on 3 4mm jet crystals, star drop, 3 4mm jet crystals. Repeat the beading pattern as shown in the photo on page 26 and adjust the beaded section so it's in the center of the necklace.

NINE • Crimp 3 wires together

String a #3 crimp bead onto 1 side of the necklace and slide the ends of 2 6" (15cm) pieces of wire inside the crimp. Use a mighty-crimp tool to crimp the crimp bead. Repeat for the other side of the necklace.

TEN • Braid wire and secure with crimp

Braid the wires together, then secure them with a #3 crimp bead. Repeat for the other side of the necklace.

ELEVEN • Attach clasp

Trim the 2 extra wires back so they're flush with the crimp bead, then attach half of the EZ-Crimp clasp to the necklace's foundation wire. (See Techniques, page 139, for instructions on using an EZ-Crimp clasp.) Repeat for the other side of the necklace.

By Fernando DaSilva

Blue Lagoon

The magnificent blue of the ocean and its gifts of pearls were my inspiration for this design. When a bracelet makes as bold a statement as this one, you can give your everyday jewelry the day off and let your wrist steal the show. Mixing several different bold elements gives this project a substantial look. The intricacy of the crystal pendants adds a flash of drama to this edgy version of a traditional pearl bracelet.

Tools

bead reamer

chain-nose pliers

round-nose pliers

mighty-crimp tool or
EZ-Crimp pliers

flush cutters

Materials

3 18mm Montana blue De Art crystal pendants

4 12mm × 8mm crystal polygon beads

1 12mm dark gray crystal pearl

2 12mm light gray crystal pearls

4 10mm light gray crystal pearls

6 8mm dark gray crystal pearls

6 6mm black diamond crystal polygon beads

5 6mm crystal comet argent cubes

4 6mm black diamond crystal cubes

10 6mm Montana blue crystal rounds

49 4mm crystal bicones

82 2mm silver shade crystal rounds

20" (51cm) .012" (.035mm) 19-strand blue stringing wire

20" (51cm) .012" (.035mm) 19-strand purple stringing wire

26 4mm silver-plated jump rings

3 silver-plated 6mm × 7.5mm oval jump rings

1 silver-plated EZ-Crimp medium toggle clasp

26 silver-plated twisted connectors

30 silver-plated head pins

30 2mm clear oval Bead Bumpers

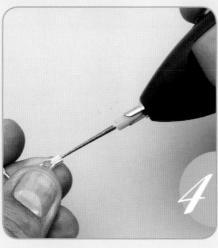

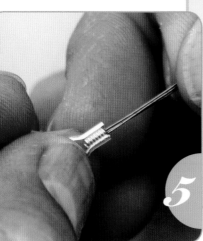

ONE • Create cube-and-connector dangles

Slide a cube and a clear Bead Bumper onto a head pin. Turn a loop above the bead and then slide a twisted connector onto the loop. Finish wrapping the loop. (See Techniques, page 140, for instructions on making a wrapped loop.) Repeat to make a total of 9 dangles.

TWO • Create round-and-connector dangles

Slide a blue round and a clear Bead Bumper onto a head pin. Link the round to a twisted connector in the same manner as in step 1. Make a total of 9 dangles. Slide a polygon bead and a clear Bead Bumper onto a head pin and make a wrapped loop above the beads. Slide the dangle onto a jump ring. Repeat to make a total of 9 dangles.

THREE • Create pendant dangles

Slide each Montana blue crystal pendant onto an oval jump ring. Link a connector to a 4mm jump ring and slide it onto the oval jump ring. Repeat with a second jump ring and connector. Make a total of 3 of these dangles. Set aside all the dangles.

FOUR • Enlarge EZ-Crimp toggle

Use a bead reamer to enlarge the opening of 1 of the EZ-Crimp toggle clasp components so it will accommodate a triple thickness of wire.

FIVE • Secure 3 strands inside EZ-Crimp end

Cut 2 10" (25cm) lengths of purple wire and 1 14" (36cm) length of blue wire. Feed all 3 wires into the EZ-Crimp end and secure them inside the EZ-Crimp end using a mighty-crimp tool.

tip

When a piece calls for lots of dangles, it's helpful to make all the dangles first. Get all the pendants ready to be hung and wait to attach them until the end. You may even want to have small trays at your jewelry station for separating pre-assembled groups of design elements.

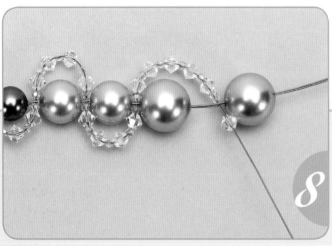

SIX • Bead first section and cross wire

String 1 8mm dark gray pearl onto the 2 purple wires together, then alternate between stringing a 2mm silver shade round and a 4mm crystal bicone onto the blue wire until there is a total of 7 beads on the blue wire. Bring the blue wire between the 2 purple strands.

SEVEN • Bead next section

String a second 8mm dark pearl onto the 2 purple wires. String 7 2mm and 4mm crystal beads onto the blue wire and bring it back between the purple wires as before, creating a wave of crystals that frames the pearls. Repeat steps 6–7 once more for a total of 3 8mm dark pearls. String a 10mm light gray pearl onto both of the purple wires and string on 9 2mm and 4mm crystal beads in the same alternating sequence described in the beginning of step 6. Repeat for 1 more 10mm light gray pearl.

EIGHT • Thread on large light gray beads

Continue stringing pearls and crystals on in the same way, this time with the following 12mm beads: 1 light gray pearl, 1 dark gray pearl, 1 light gray pearl. Thread the blue strand with smaller crystals, framing each large pearl with 11 2mm and 4mm crystal beads. Finish beading the bracelet in reverse order. Insert all 3 wires into the remaining EZ-Crimp toggle component and squeeze it closed with chain-nose pliers. Trim away the excess wire.

NINE • Attach dangles

Link each polygon dangle from step 2 to a 4mm jump ring. Link 1 cube-and-connector dangle and 1 round-and-connector dangle to a single jump ring. Repeat until you've created 9 dangles. Attach all the dangles to different points in the bracelet as you like. Close all the jump rings carefully. *Voilá!* You are ready for the cat walk!

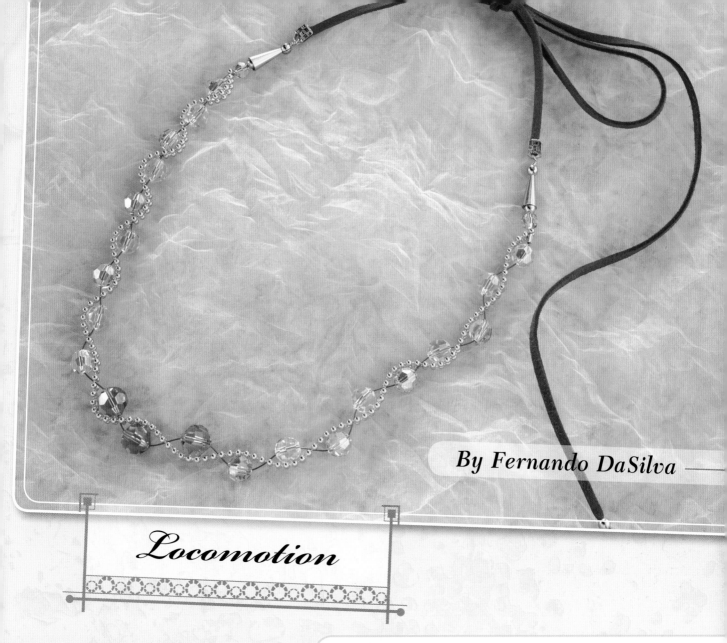

By Fernando DaSilva

Locomotion

Since I was a little kid I have been fascinated by railroads. The image of a road made of rocks and iron snaking through the geography of different lands is a constant in my mind. In this piece, I translated the image of a freight train carrying precious metal and gemstones into an eye-catching necklace. The intricate double-ball chain plays the role of the railroad and the magical crystallized version of cognac and pink diamonds fits my childhood daydreams like a glove.

Materials

3 10mm light Colorado topaz crystal rounds

10 8mm gold shade crystal rounds

8 8mm silk crystal rounds

2 6mm gold shade crystal rounds

2' (.6m) gold-plated double-ball chain

1' (.3m) 24-gauge gold-plated German-style wire

.018" (.045mm) red-plated 19-strand beading wire

30" (76cm) red faux suede lace cord

2 gold-plated necklace cones

2 gold-plated C-crimp ends

6 4mm copper crimp covers

2 #2 gold-plated crimp tubes

2 #3 gold-plated crimp tubes

Tools

flush cutters

chain-nose pliers

round-nose pliers

crimp pliers

mighty-crimp pliers

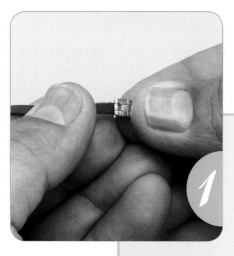

ONE • Attach fold-over end to cord

Cut 2 22" (56cm) lengths of red faux suede lace cord. Slip an end of 1 of the faux suede pieces into a C-crimp end and use chain-nose pliers to crimp the C closed, securing the faux suede. Repeat for 1 end of the other length of cord.

TWO • Secure a loop at end of wire with crimp tube

Form a loop at 1 end of a 20" (51cm) strand of red wire by stringing a #2 crimp tube onto the end of the wire, then bringing the wire back through the crimp. Secure the crimp with crimping pliers. (See Techniques, page 138, for instructions on using a crimp tube.) Trim away the excess wire end with flush cutters.

THREE • Thread double-ball chain and crimp tube onto wire

String a 6mm crystal gold shade round bead onto the red wire. Then thread on the double-ball chain, feeding the wire through the first square opening in the chain. String on 1 #3 crimp tube and crimp it next to the chain as close as possible. Make sure not to string the wire too tightly through the chain. A loose weave creates a better flow.

FOUR • Creat first curved section

String 1 8mm gold shade bead onto the red wire. Count to the 6th opening in the chain and feed the wire through this opening. The chain should begin to wrap the outer portion of the first bead.

FIVE • String necklace

String on 1 8mm silk bead, count 6 more openings in the double-ball chain and feed the wire through the 6th opening. Continue in this same manner, alternating between gold shade and silk rounds until you have strung 5 gold shade rounds and 4 silk rounds. At the center of the necklace, string on 3 10mm light Colorado topaz beads, weaving the ball chain around them in the same manner as with the smaller beads, counting 7 openings in the chain to accommodate the larger beads. Bead the remaining half of the necklace in the same manner as the first half, including the 2 crimp tubes (see steps 2 and 3).

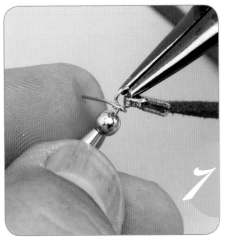

SIX • Link beaded section to gold wire

Cover the final crimp tube on each side of the strung necklace with a copper crimp cover. Use the mighty-crimp tool to secure the covers. (See Techniques, page 138, for instructions on using a crimp cover.) Cut 2 6" (15cm) lengths of 24-gauge gold-plated German-style wire. Slide 1 end of a piece of the wire through 1 of the red wire loops and bend it into a loop. Wrap the tail of the wire around the base of the loop. (See Techniques, page 140, for instructions on making a wrapped loop.) Trim away the excess wire with flush cutters.

SEVEN • Link suede to beaded strand

Slide a gold-plated necklace cone onto the wire. Secure a copper crimp cover above the cone. Turn a loop above the crimp cover and thread 1 of the C-crimps onto the wire. Wrap the wire around itself carefully twice to secure 1 side of the necklace. Cut away the excess wire with flush cutters and tuck the remaining wire flat. Repeat steps 6 and 7 to secure the opposite side of the necklace.

EIGHT • Secure leather with crimp cover

Measure approximately 20" (51cm) from the C-crimp along the faux suede and place a crimp cover there. Secure it with the mighty-crimp tool. Repeat for the other side of the necklace.

NINE • Trim leather

Use flush cutters to trim the faux suede flush with the top of each crimp cover.

Black and Gold Locomotion

For this version, I used gold-plated double-ball chain combined with jet and black diamond crystal. Changing up the color of the beads and the suede lace completely alters the look of this design. Experiment with your favorite color combinations!

2 Precious Metals
Designs Featuring Metallic Wire

The flash of metal combined with the sparkle of crystal creates a thoroughly enchanting effect. Is it the cool, sleek, sophisticated vibe of the metallic wire or is it the glamorous, effervescent, mysterious aura of the crystal? It's hard to be certain, but together the two are positively divine! In this chapter you'll find architecturally inspired exposed metal-wire creations combined with crystal beads and components in totally unexpected ways. The more you play with these techniques, the more inspired you will be to explore your own three-dimensional designs with wire and crystal.

Make sure you try out all of these ideas and see how they spark new directions in your work. Take on the *Zigzagged* necklace (see page 42) for a quirky new twist on the looped wire idea. *Silver Splendor* (see page 47) is a fireworks-like display of metal and crystal that you can easily dress up or down depending on the beads you use. Try out the *Galactic Waves* necklace (see page 44) for an haute couture runway feel and think about what other pendants you could use to beautifully set off this design.

By Margot Potter

Concentricity

Want to make a bracelet that's as light as air? Pair wire circles in varied sizes with beads and bits that slip and slide around your wrist to create a playfully pretty design. It's easy as pi. Hee. Wire circles offer endless design possibilities. Bead them up or leave them sparse so the beads can move freely along the wire. I can't stop making these circles and coming up with new ways to use them.

Materials

7 4mm red coral crystal rounds

7 4mm mint alabaster crystal rounds

7 4mm white alabaster crystal rounds

6 4mm rose water opal crystal rounds

.018" (.45mm) Satin Gold wire

14 5mm gold-plated jump rings

1 small gold-toggle clasp

5 gold-plated center-hole discs

8 gold-plated #2 crimp beads

8 gold-plated crimp covers

3 gold-plated head pins

Tools

round-nose pliers

chain-nose pliers

mighty-crimp tool

wire cutters

Silver Concentricity

The same design created with satin silver wire paired with white alabaster, violet opal, rose water opal, silver and lime beads and silver-plated beaded rings, hearts and ovals has a totally different vibe. The more you play with color, the more you expand your aesthetic in exciting new directions.

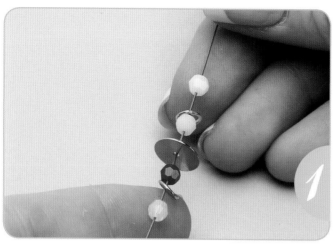

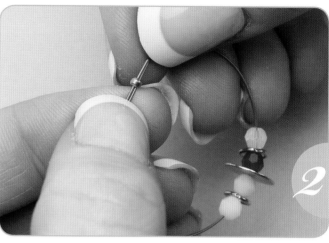

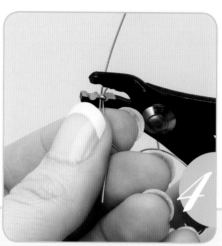

ONE • Thread beads onto wire
Cut 4 4" (10cm) and 4 3" (8cm) segments of Satin Gold wire. Thread a white alabaster round, a jump ring, a mint alabaster round, a center-drilled disc, a red coral round, a jump ring and a rose water opal onto the longer wire segment.

TWO • Crimp wire circle
While holding the beads to keep them in place on the wire, thread each end of the wire into a crimp tube from opposite sides, forming a circle. Grasp both wires and keep them uncrossed as you crimp the bead in place. (See Techniques, page 138, for instructions on securing a crimp bead.) Use wire cutters to trim away the excess wire. This circle should be approximately 1" (3cm) in diameter when finished.

THREE • Link next wire circle
Thread a 3" (8cm) wire segment with a mint alabaster round, a gold disc and a white alabaster round. Thread the wire through the first circle, again securing the wire circle with a crimp bead as in step 2.

FOUR • Continue linking beaded wire circles
Add a large beaded circle as in step 2, following the same beading pattern as in step 1. Bead the next small circle in the following sequence: rose water opal round, jump ring and red coral round. Continue alternating large and small circles and alternating the bead pattern in the small circles for a total of 8 circles.

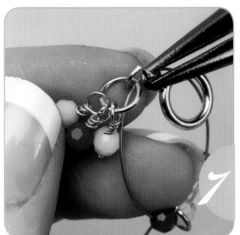

FIVE • Cover crimp beads with crimp covers

Cover each crimp tube with a crimp cover by sliding it over the tube and using the round end of the mighty-crimp tool to compress the bead shut, concealing the tube.

SIX • Attach clasp components

Attach the O ring of a toggle clasp to the small circle on 1 side of your bracelet using a jump ring. Attach the bar end of your toggle to the other end of the bracelet with a chain of 2 jump rings, allowing the bar to pass through the circle more easily.

SEVEN • Add dangles

Create 3 beaded dangles by sliding each of the following beads onto a head pin and making a wrapped loop above each bead: 1 red coral, 1 mint alabaster and 1 alabaster. (See Techniques, page 140, for instructions on making a wrapped loop.) Slide all 3 dangles onto a jump ring. Link the 3 dangles to the connecting jump ring at your circle toggle end.

By Margot Potter

Zigzagged

Wires and crystals dodge and dart around your neck
in a carefree manner in this thoroughly modern
design. The citrus colors are redolent of a day at the
beach, but you can switch the mood by changing
them up any way you please. Try making more
strands, layers of strands, a bib effect, a bracelet
. . . whatever your heart desires. Wear this for those
moments when you want to feel mysterious; will you
zig, will you zag? One never knows, does one?

Materials

11 9mm × 6mm erinite crystal briolettes
64 6mm chrysolite crystal bicones
62 6mm jonquil crystal bicones
.018" (.45mm) 49-strand silver-plated wire
11 4mm silver-plated jump rings
6 6mm silver-plated jump rings
1 small silver-plated toggle clasp
6 EZ-Crimp ends

Tools

round-nose pliers

2 pairs chain-nose pliers

EZ-Crimp pliers

wire cutters

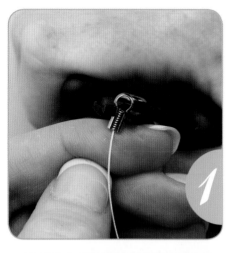

ONE • Attach first strand of wire to EZ-Crimp end

Cut a 54" (137cm) length of silver-plated wire. Feed the wire end into an EZ-Crimp end and squeeze it closed. (See Techniques, page 139, for instructions on using an EZ-Crimp end.)

TWO • Begin to make first beaded loop

String 2 6mm chrysolite bicones onto the wire. Bring the wire end back through the beads from the top and begin pulling the wire through the second bead.

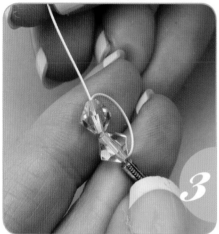

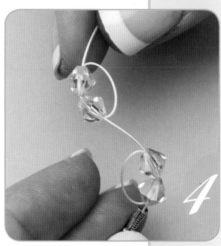

THREE • Finish first beaded loop

Continue pulling on the wire until you've created a loop, making sure the beads are flush with the EZ-Crimp end.

FOUR • Bead all 3 strands

String on 2 6mm jonquil bicones and loop them in place approximately ⅜" to ½" (1cm to 2cm) below the first pair of beads. Continue looping beads onto the first strand, alternating between pairs of chrysolite and jonquil bicones until there are 21 pairs of beads. Repeat with 2 more 54" (137cm) strands of silver-plated wire. 2 of the strands should begin and end with chrysolite beads, and 1 strand should begin and end with jonquil beads.

FIVE • Add dangles

Working with 1 of the strands beginning and ending with chrysolite beads, attach an erinite briolette with a 4mm jump ring to the loop with each pair of chrysolite beads. (See Techniques, page 141, for instructions on opening and closing a jump ring.) Repeat to add a briolette dangle to each pair of chrysolite beads on that strand.

SIX • Link crimp ends to jump rings

Attach an EZ-Crimp end to the end of each wire, pulling the beads flush with the crimp end. Attach all 3 ends on 1 side to a 6mm jump ring. Repeat for the other side. Attach the O ring portion of the clasp to an end of the necklace with a 6mm jump ring. Attach the bar end of the clasp to the other end of the necklace with a chain of 3 jump rings. Check all the jump rings to make sure they're securely closed.

By Fernando DaSilva

Galactic Waves

The desire to make an ultra-modern, curvy multilayered necklace using silver-plated wire led me to experiment with a wire twister on this design. The result is absolutely astonishing. I added the Galactic pendant by CRYSTALLIZED – *Swarovski Elements* to complement the futuristic look of the bare, twisting wire.

Materials

1 23.5mm × 39mm crystal Galactic horizontal pendant

23 2mm crystal moonlight rounds

8 2mm jet crystal rounds

.024" (.61mm) 49-strand silver-plated stringing wire

.013" (.33mm) 49-strand silver-plated stringing wire

20-gauge German-style stringing wire

3 6mm sterling silver jump rings

1 medium sterling silver lobster clasp

20 #3 silver-plated crimp tubes

1 #1 silver-plated crimp tube

2 sterling silver bead caps (available from Rio Grande)

Tools

round-nose pliers

chain-nose pliers

standard crimping pliers

micro-crimp tool

wire twister tool

wire cutters

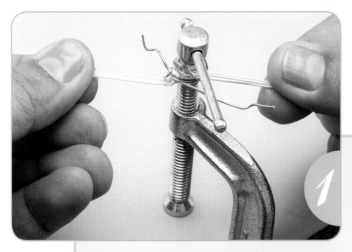

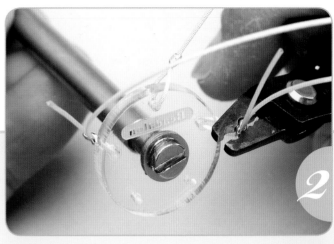

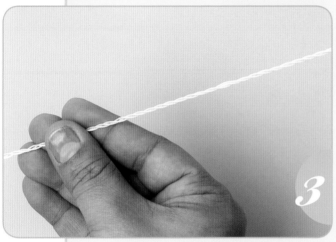

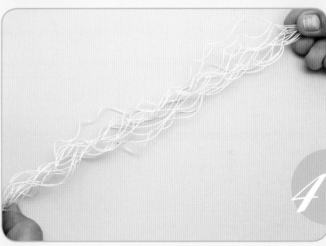

ONE • Attach wire to a stationary object

Cut 6 40" (102cm) lengths of .024" (.61mm) 49-strand silver-plated stringing wire. Tie 3 of the strands into a knot at 1 end. Form a large loop with German-style wire and use it to attach the silver-plated wire to a stationary object, such as a chair or table leg, or a vise clamped to a table top.

TWO • Secure wire to twist tool with crimps

Crimp the free end of each piece of wire to 1 of the holes in the wire twister. (See Techniques, page 138, for instructions on securing a crimp tube.)

THREE • Twist wire

Twist the crank of the wire twister while keeping tension on the wires. Keep twisting until the wires start to show a permanent "wave." More twisting will make smaller waves.

FOUR • Twist remaining strands

Cut off the crimps and the wires at the twisting tool. Repeat steps 1, 2 and 3 to make 13 total strands of twisted wire.

tip

This project is challenging. I made three versions before I was pleased with the results. Remember that originally the wire twister was created to wrap wire. I decided to experiment with the tool using beading wire, so it's natural that the results can be unpredictable. Persistence is the key to this project.

FIVE • String twisted wires onto wire loop

Cut a 4" (10cm) piece of German-style wire and shape it into a loop that is just small enough to fit into a bead cap using the thickest point of the round-nose pliers. Make the loop at 1 end of the wire, and leave a long tail of approximately 3" (8cm). Make a small loop at 1 end of each strand and secure it with a crimp tube. String all 13 strands, 1 by 1, onto the German-style wire loop. Before wrapping the loop closed, make sure everything will fit inside the end cap. Make any necessary adjustments, then wrap the loop closed and trim away any excess wire. (See Techniques, page 140, for instructions on making a wrapped loop.)

SIX • Secure wires inside bead cap

Thread the German-style wire into the bead cap and pull the wires snug inside, hiding the crimp tubes.

SEVEN • Attach clasp

Make a loop above the bead cap. Open a 6mm jump ring and slide the lobster clasp onto it. Close the jump ring. (See Techniques, page 141, for instructions on opening and closing a jump ring.) Slide the jump ring onto the wire loop. Wrap the loop closed. Trim away the excess wire. Repeat steps 5–7 for the other end of the necklace.

EIGHT • Begin beaded bail

Cut a 12" (31cm) piece of .013" (.33mm) silver-plated wire. String 3 2mm moonlight beads and 1 2mm jet crystal bead onto the wire. Continue stringing in this pattern until there are 6 jet crystal beads on the wire. Then string on a crimp tube. Slide the Galactic crystal pendant onto the beaded strand. Bring the wire ends through the crimp tube in opposite directions, creating a circle. Begin pulling on the wire ends to tighten the circle into a beaded bail.

NINE • Finish beaded bail

Continue tightening the bail until the beads form a continuous circle. Secure the bail by flattening the crimp tube using the micro-crimp tool. Cut away any excess wire with wire cutters.

Silver Splendor

There is more to this necklace than meets the eye. The central piece of beading wire runs through the entire design, but extra strands are braided onto the sides to create a decorative effect. You build the necklace from the center out, which allows you to experiment with different lengths of fringe and to add as many dimensional wires as you desire.

Tools

standard crimping pliers

mighty-crimp tool

wire cutters

Materials

5 9mm x 6mm jet top-drilled crystal briolettes

12 8mm jet crystal cubes

41 6mm jet crystal bicones

61 4mm crystal AB crystal rounds

.015" (.38mm) 49-strand silver-plated wire

.024" (.61mm) 49-strand silver-plated wire

1 sterling silver S-hook EZ-Crimp clasp

4 silver crimp covers

51 #1 silver crimp beads

4 #3 silver crimp beads

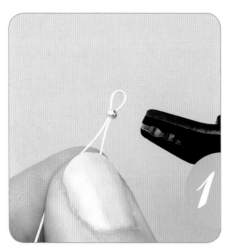

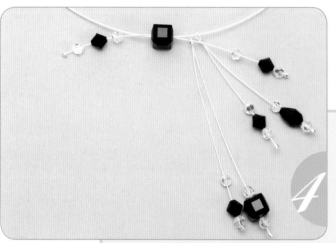

ONE • Fold wire and crimp in place
Cut the following lengths of .024" (.61mm) beading wire: 1 16½" (42cm) piece and 2 5½" (14cm) pieces. Cut the following lengths of .015" (.38mm) beading wire: 1 6" (15cm) piece, 2 5" (13cm) pieces, 4 3½" (9cm) pieces, 6 3" (8cm) pieces, 10 2½" (6cm) pieces. Fold the 6" (15cm) piece of wire in half and thread a crimp bead onto both strands. Slide the crimp bead up the wires to ⅛" (6mm) from the fold. Use a crimping tool to attach the crimp bead. (See Techniques, page 138, for instructions on using a crimp bead.)

TWO • Create first tassel
String a crystal round and a jet bicone onto 1 end of the folded 6" (15cm) wire. Thread a crimp bead onto the very tip of the wire and attach it with a crimp tool to secure the beads. String a crystal round and a different jet bead onto the other end of the wire. Crimp those beads in place as well. Repeat steps 1 and 2 to make 2 beaded tassels with the 5" (13cm) pieces of wire and 4 tassels with the 3½" (9cm) pieces of wire.

THREE • String small wire piece through strung bead
String a cube onto the center of the 16½" (42cm) strand of beading wire. Pass a 3" (8cm) piece of wire through the cube. String a crystal round, jet bicone and another crystal round onto each protruding wire end. Secure the beads in place with crimp beads.

FOUR • String on tassels
String a 6" (15cm) and 5" (13cm) piece of fringe onto 1 side of the center cube.

FIVE • Slide on bead
String a jet bicone onto the wire.

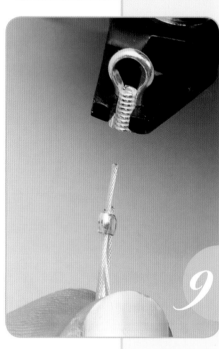

SIX • String necklace and secure wires

Pass a 3" (8cm) piece of wire through the bicone and add the beads of your choice to the ends. String on a 3½" (9cm) fringe and a cube bead. Pass a 3" (8cm) piece of wire through the cube bead and add beads to the ends. String on a 3½" (9cm) fringe and a bicone. Pass a 2½" (6cm) piece of wire through the bicone and add beads.

String on 2 more cubes, alternating with 2 bicones, and passing 2½" (6cm) wires through each bead. Add beads to the wire ends. Repeat to string the other side of the necklace, beginning with a single 5" (13cm) fringe. String a crystal bead and a #3 crimp bead onto the wire.

Adjust the beaded section so it's centered on the 16½" (42cm) wire. Cut 2 5½" (14cm) lengths of .024" (.61mm) beading wire and place the ends inside the #3 crimp bead. Crimp the crimp bead, making sure all 3 strands are securely in place. Slide a crimp cover over the flattened crimp and use a mighty-crimp tool to close it. (See Techniques, page 138, for instructions on using crimp covers.)

SEVEN • Braid wire strands

Braid the strands together.

EIGHT • Attach clasp

Attach a #3 crimp bead to the ends, making sure you can tell which wire is the original 16½" (42cm) strand. Cut off any extra wire on the strands that were added in step 6, then cover the crimp with a crimp cover.

NINE • Finish necklace

Trim the end of the original 16½" (42cm) wire to ¼" (6mm) above the crimp cover. Attach an EZ-Crimp end to the end of the wire. (See Techniques, page 139, for instructions on securing an EZ-Crimp end.) Repeat to finish the other side of the necklace. Attach an S-hook clasp to the EZ-Crimp end.

By Katie Hacker

Classic Combination

Double needle weaving is one of my favorite techniques. It's easy to do and it attracts a lot of compliments. For this bracelet, I wanted to mimic the look and feel of gemstones. Turquoise, Caribbean blue opal and dark red coral crystals work together in a very classic color palette, but the scallop design gives it an unexpected twist. Silver-plated beading wire makes the bracelet supple and strong, and it adds a delightful bit of metallic shine.

Materials

9 8mm Caribbean blue opal flat crystal briolettes

50 6mm dark red coral crystal rounds

126 4mm Caribbean blue opal crystal rounds

140 4mm turquoise crystal bicones

.015" (.38mm) silver-plated 49-strand beading wire

2-strand silver slide clasp

4 #2 silver crimp beads

4 4mm silver crimp covers

adhesive tape or stopper beads

Tools

standard crimping pliers

mighty-crimp tool or EZ-Crimp pliers

wire cutters

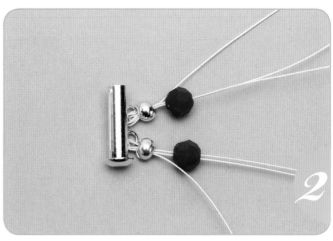

ONE • Crimp wires to clasp

Cut 6 18" (46cm) lengths of beading wire. Holding 3 wires together, pass them through a crimp bead, through a loop on the clasp and back into the crimp bead. Use standard crimping pliers to crimp the crimp bead. Place a crimp cover over the crimp and use a mighty-crimp tool to close it. (See Techniques, page 138, for instructions on securing wire with a crimp tube and securing a crimp cover.) Repeat to attach 3 more wires to the other loop on the same half of the clasp.

TWO • String on coral rounds

Isolate 1 wire from each set, moving each wire to the side. Hold 2 wires together and string on a 6mm dark red coral crystal. Repeat for the other set of wires.

THREE • Pass both sets of wires through center bead

Pass each set of 2 wires through a 6mm dark red coral round, bringing them through the bead in opposite directions.

FOUR • String on first Caribbean blue briolette

Isolate 1 wire from each set, moving it to the side. Thread a 6mm dark red coral crystal onto each working wire. Pass each wire through an 8mm Caribbean blue opal briolette, bringing them through the bead in opposite directions. Using the same 2 wires, repeat the beading pattern 8 more times. Pass each wire end through a final dark red coral crystal, then secure the wire ends with adhesive tape or stopper beads.

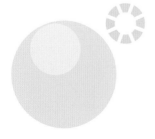

FIVE • String on turquoise bicones

String 7 turquoise bicones onto 1 of the wires closest to the clasp. Repeat for the corresponding wire. Pass 1 of the wires through the first 8mm Caribbean blue briolette to create a scallop. Repeat for the corresponding wire, bringing it through the briolette from the first strand in the opposite direction. Repeat this step 7 more times, then string 7 turquoise bicones onto each wire and cover the wire ends with tape or use stopper beads.

SIX • String on Caribbean blue rounds

Pick up the remaining empty wires and string 7 4mm Caribbean blue opal rounds onto each wire. Pass the wires through opposite sides of the next dark red coral crystal. Repeat this step to create 8 more scallops, each positioned between 2 turquoise scallops. Pass each wire end through the corresponding last dark red coral crystal on the bracelet.

SEVEN • Finish bracelet

Attach a set of 3 wire ends to each loop on the clasp, just as in step 1. Make any necessary adjustments to the scallops, pull the wire ends taut and make sure the clasp is oriented in the proper direction before attaching the crimps.

Monochromatic Combination

This bracelet looks great in a variety of color combinations. For a subtler effect, try a monochromatic color scheme like this purple velvet and violet opal version. Experiment with beading wire colors, too, but remember to use 49-strand, the most flexible beading wire.

Listening to music is a source of daily inspiration for me. One day the refrain from Elton John's song "Empty Garden" got stuck in my head. I started thinking about what my

make one for yourself and experiment.

By Fernando DaSilva

Twisted Garden

Materials

1 21mm burgundy crystal polygon drop

4 17mm burgundy crystal polygon drops

10 15.4mm × 14mm ruby flat crystal briolettes

33 13mm × 6.5mm rose alabaster crystal briolettes

38 13mm × 6.5mm Siam crystal briolettes

55 9mm × 5mm moonlight crystal briolettes

20 6mm top-drilled rose crystal bicone pendants

.018" (.45mm) 19-strand satin silver beading wire

.024" (.61mm) 19-strand sterling silver beading wire

.024" (.61mm) 49-strand silver-plated beading wire

2 6mm silver-plated jump rings

1 6mm sterling silver jump ring

1 set sterling silver 3-strand EZ-Crimp toggle clasp

2 sterling silver EZ-Crimp ends

10 silver-plated pinch bails

Detachable Drops

1 21mm burgundy crystal polygon drop

2 15.4mm × 14mm ruby flat crystal briolettes

5 13mm × 6.5mm rose alabaster crystal briolettes

4 13mm × 6.5mm Siam crystal briolettes

5 9mm × 5mm moonlight crystal briolettes

6 6mm top-drilled rose crystal bicone pendants

10 6mm silver-plated jump rings

3 4mm silver-plated jump rings

3 medium silver-plated EZ-Lobster Clasps

3 silver-plated pinch bails

Tools

chain-nose pliers

mighty-crimp tool or EZ-Crimp pliers

crimp tool

wire cutters

ONE • Attach 3 strands to EZ-Crimp ends

Insert a 26" (66cm) piece of satin silver beading wire inside an EZ-Crimp end on the 3-strand toggle. Place the smooth portion of the EZ-Crimp end inside EZ-Crimp pliers and squeeze until the coiled section of the EZ-Crimp end begins to close down around the beading wire. This will be called strand A. Secure another 26" (66cm) strand of satin silver beading wire (strand B). Secure a 26" (66cm) strand of sterling silver beading wire in the final EZ-Crimp end (strand C). Attach a jump ring to the O ring. (See Techniques, page 141, for instructions on opening and closing a jump ring.)

TWO • Bead first section

Now get ready! Loosen your shoulders and relax because the flight might be bumpy—but we will land safely. Randomly string on all the crystal elements, spacing the flat briolettes evenly every 2" (5cm) or so.

THREE • Continue beading

Continue beading the necklace with a random assortment of crystals. String some crystals on just 1 strand, string others on 2 strands and bring the wires across each other to create interesting effects.

FOUR • Bead center of necklace

At the center of the necklace, after beading approximately 7¼" (18cm), string on 2 9mm × 5mm moonlight crystal briolettes, followed by a 21mm burgundy polygon drop and 3 more moonlight crystal briolettes, crossing the wires as you string and stringing some beads onto 1 wire and others onto 2 wires. Bead the second half of the necklace with a random assortment of crystals. Attach the other half of the toggle clasp as in step 1.

Twisted Garden Earrings

Complete the fabulous look of this necklace with equally fabulous earrings. Using a two-ring circle connector, pick up the colors of the necklace for a luscious look. Either a post with ring or lever-backs will work, depending on your preference. The use of a connector will ensure the movement of your earrings, creating the feeling of a sensuous summer afternoon.

FIVE • Weave in fourth beaded strand

Cut another 26" (66cm) strand of silver-plated wire. Secure the wire to the O ring with an EZ-Crimp end linked to a 4mm jump ring. String 3 6mm rose crystal top-drilled bicone pendants (or any 3 top-drilled beads) onto the wire, then feed the wire through a bead about 1" (3cm) from the first grouping. String on 3 more top-drilled beads of your choice and string the wire through a bead about 1" (3cm) from this grouping. String on another grouping of crystals as before.

SIX • Pull beaded strand snug

After stringing on a few groupings of crystals, pause to pull the strand taut, nestling the groupings of beads into the main beaded strands.

SEVEN • Create detachable dangle

Slide a pinch bail into a ruby flat briolette and squeeze the pinch bail closed. Link the pinch bail to a 4mm jump ring. Link a 6mm jump ring to the 4mm jump ring. Open a 6mm jump ring and thread on a rose bicone pendant, a rose alabaster briolette and a moonlight crystal briolette. Link the jump ring to the other 6mm jump ring. Open another 6mm jump ring and thread on a 17mm burgundy polygon drop and a moonlight crystal briolette. Link this jump ring to the jump ring attached to the 4mm ring. Link a lobster clasp to the jump ring with the polygon drop. Use the clasp to attach the dangle to the O ring. Use your imagination here and make multiple detachable dangles. See the additional dangles below for more ideas.

Detachable Dangles

Use any leftover crystal elements to create multiple detachable dangles. The idea is to spotlight one main color in each drop—this is a great opportunity to play around and use your imagination.

Shape Shifters
Designs Featuring Colourcraft Shaping Wire

Hard shaping wire can be wrapped, curled, curved and manipulated into all sorts of intriguing geometries. Adding crystal to hard wire designs gives them a glamorous edge. This chapter gives you interesting twists on using shaping wire and some innovative new ideas. From a playful wire-wrapped necklace (see page 66) to a totally over-the-top tiara (see page 58), we've got you covered in this chapter. Get out your wire and your imagination and try on some new tools, tricks, tips and techniques for size. You'll be wired for speed before you know it.

You really won't believe all the things you can do with shaping wire. Learn how to make your own gorgeous twisted jump rings when you make the *Simply Charming* bracelet (see page 60). With its fiery red wire loops combined with crystal bling, this bracelet is sure to turn some heads. Explore the technique of wrapping crystals around a wire base to make the classy *Triptych* earrings (see page 70).

The fluid lines of these crystal starfish, along with their considerable size and presence, make them perfectly suited to one of my favorite jewelry-making projects—a tiara! I started with the idea of creating a mermaid's crown and played around with different bead shapes, colors and sizes to find the perfect balance. The crystal satin beads have a very watery, magical feel. The starfish are set off by regal opaque palace green opal beads and seaweed-green biwa-style crystal pearls that mimic the fluidity of the focal beads.

By Margot Potter

Mermaid Queen

Materials

1 40mm crystal AB starfish

2 28mm crystal AB starfish

6 9mm × 8mm cream rose biwa crystal pearls

12 8mm palace green opal crystal rounds

10 8mm satin crystal rounds

1 Goody's metal headband

22-gauge German-style beading wire

Tools

wire cutters

Royal Earrings

Wrap galactic beads with gold wire and link them to satin and green opal rounds to make a regal pair of earrings to match your tiara.

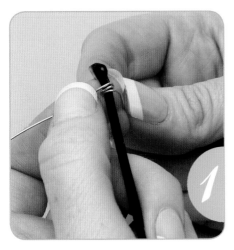

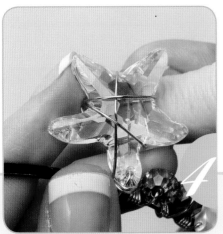

ONE • Begin to wrap wire

Remove as much wire from the coil as you can comfortably work with without introducing kinks or loops. (Note: I use about 4' [1.2m] of wire. If you like, use less wire and patch in the new wire as you work.) Begin on the right side of the tiara (which would be on the left side of your head if you were wearing it). Wrap the wire over the top of the band, grasping the tail of the wire to create tension as you begin to coil the wire.

TWO • Wrap on beads

Wrap the wire around the headband for 1½" (4cm). String a satin round onto the wire. Wrap the wire around the band 5 times, starting as close to the satin bead as possible. Add a palace green opal round and secure it by wrapping the wire around the band 5 times. Continue wrapping beads onto the headband with 5 wraps between each bead in the following 4-bead pattern: satin round, palace green opal round, pearl, green opal. Then wrap on 1 satin round.

THREE • Begin to wrap starfish

Thread a 28mm starfish onto the wire and wrap the wire around the band twice. Wrap the wire around the wire beneath the starfish twice.

FOUR • Crisscross wire around starfish

Bring the wire up and around several of the starfish arms, crisscrossing the wire and wrapping the wire around the starfish a total of 4 times, keeping the wire taut to create the right amount of tension. Finish wrapping the starfish by wrapping the wire around the band, around the bottom of the wire twice as in step 3 and back around the base.

FIVE • Continue wrapping beads

Wrap on 1 full 4-bead pattern plus 1 more satin round, keeping 5 coils between beads. At the center of the headband, wrap the 40mm starfish in place using the technique in steps 3 and 4.

SIX • Finish tiara

Wrap on another 4-bead pattern plus 1 more satin round. Wrap on a second 28mm starfish. Finish the tiara with 2 more 4-bead sequences and end with 1 satin round. Wrap the wire around the base tightly until you reach the end of the base. Use wire cutters to cut off any excess wire and tuck it flush to the back of the base.

By Katie Hacker

Simply Charming

Make your own charm bracelet from scratch with this twisted-wire jump ring technique. The connected rings form a chain that's beautiful and durable. Choose a wire color that complements your components, then add beaded charms and dangles for a sweet, swingy finish.

Materials

3 20mm crystal stars

3 14mm crystal/silver crystal flowers

3 8mm light Siam crystal rounds

3 4mm AB crystal rounds

3 Siam crystal channels

24-gauge red craft wire

20-gauge red craft wire

3 6mm silver jump rings

3 4mm silver jump rings

16mm silver toggle clasp

3 silver head pins

3 silver eye pins

Tools

jump ring maker with 4mm and 8mm mandrels

wire twister

chain-nose pliers

round-nose pliers

wire cutters

Charming Bracelet

If you don't have time to make your own wire chain but you love the look, use thick polyester chain instead. The heavy links create a similar effect and make a great foundation for adding beaded charms and dangles.

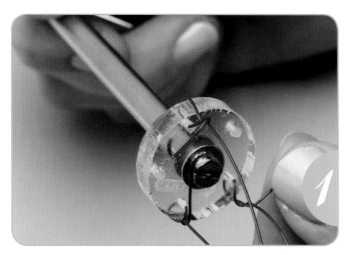

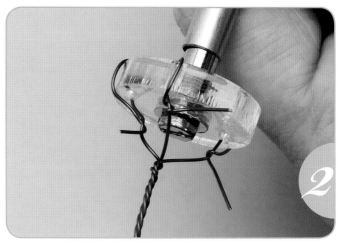

For a quicker version, use premade chain instead of making the twisted rings. Or substitute sterling or gold-filled wire for the red wire, and use precious metal charms to coordinate. You can even easily transform this bracelet into a necklace. Simply connect lengths of ribbon or cord to the ends and your necklace is finished.

tip

ONE • Prepare to twist wire

Cut 3 3-yard (2.7m) lengths of red craft wire. Wrap each wire end around a stationary object such as a clamp or a doorknob. Attach each wire to a hole on the twister, making sure the wires remain about the same length. If 1 wire is longer than another, it will create a bump in the twist.

TWO • Twist wires

Hold the shaft and turn the handle to complete the twist. By twisting the pieces of craft wire together, you're actually work-hardening the wire. Hardening the wire forces the molecules of the metal closer together and creates a very tight twist that won't easily unravel. Keep twisting until the wire breaks, then cut the other end to remove it from the clamp or twisting tool.

THREE • Wrap twisted wire around mandrel

Attach the 8mm mandrel to the plastic base, straighten 1 wire end and thread it through the hole on the jump ring maker. Turn the handle to form a long coil.

FOUR • Cut coiled wire into rings

Remove the coil from the jump ring maker and use wire cutters to cut the rings apart.
Make a total of 54 rings. Separate them into 18 groupings of 3.

FIVE • Link jump rings

Link each group of 3 jump rings to another group of 3 jump rings. (See Techniques, page
141, for instructions on opening and closing a jump ring.) Continue until you've used all
54 jump rings.

SIX • Make dangles

Make 3 each of the following 3 dangles: Slide an AB crystal round onto a head pin and
turn a loop above the bead. (See Techniques, page 140, for instructions on turning a
loop.) Connect a 4mm ring to the top loop in the Siam channel. For the second set of
dangles, slide a light Siam round onto an eye pin and turn a loop above the bead. Link
the dangle to 1 loop on a crystal flower. To create the third set of dangles, simply slide
a crystal star onto a 6mm jump ring. Taking care to work on 1 side of the bracelet, link a
dangle to the bottom ring in every other set of jump rings.

SEVEN • Add clasp

Cut a 6" (15cm) length of 20-gauge red wire and wrap it around the 4mm mandrel to form
a short coil. Cut 4 rings off of the coil. Use 2 red jump rings to connect half of the clasp
to each end of the bracelet.

By Katie Hacker

Copper Droplets

Exposed wire spirals form the foundation of this swirly necklace design. It's an ancient technique made new again with the addition of velvety velour tubing and sparkly crystal pendants. You can make the spirals by hand using nylon-jaw pliers, or give the new spiral-making tool a whirl. Get your spiral on with this sophisticated design!

Materials

3 20mm crystal copper avant garde crystal pendants

6 4mm light Colorado topaz crystal rounds

.018" (.45mm) 19-strand satin copper beading wire

20-gauge brown craft wire

24-gauge copper craft wire

brown velour tubing

3 6mm copper jump rings

10mm copper toggle clasp

4 #1 crimp beads

4 4mm copper crimp covers

Tools

spiral maker

round-nose pliers

chain-nose pliers

standard crimping pliers

wire cutters

ONE • Begin to create spiral

Cut 4 12" (31cm) lengths of brown craft wire. Place an end of a 12" (31cm) piece of wire inside the spiral maker and turn the handle to form a spiral, using approximately 6" (15cm) of the wire.

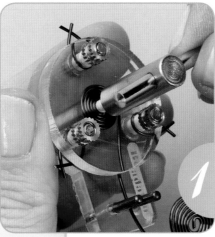

TWO • Finish double spiral

Carefully remove the spiral and place the other end of the wire inside the tool. Turn the handle to form a spiral facing the opposite direction from the first spiral. Keep turning the handle until the 2 spirals meet. Repeat steps 1 and 2 to make 3 more double spirals.

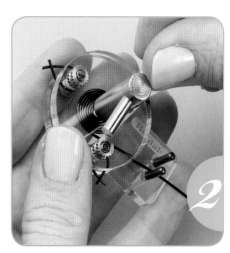

THREE • Link copper wire to first double spiral

Connect a jump ring to each crystal copper pendant. (See Techniques, page 141, for instructions on opening and closing a jump ring.) Set them aside. Cut a 3" (8cm) length of copper wire and fold up 1" (3cm) of 1 end. Pass the folded wire through the center of a spiral and make a wrapped loop on the outside of the spiral to secure it. (See Techniques, page 140, for instructions on making a wrapped loop.)

FOUR • String on beads

String the following beads onto the wire: 4mm crystal, crystal copper pendant, 4mm crystal. Link the beaded section to the next double spiral in the same manner as in step 3. Repeat steps 4–5 to connect the remaining double spirals to form the center of the necklace.

FIVE • Attach sides of necklace to central section

Cut a piece of copper beading wire to about 8" (20cm). Link the wire to an end double spiral with a crimp bead. (See Techniques, page 138, for instructions on securing wire with crimp beads.) Secure a crimp cover over the flattened bead. (See Techniques, page 138, for instructions on using a crimp cover.)

SIX • Finish necklace

Cut a piece of velour tubing 1" (3cm) shorter than the beading wire. Pass the wire through the tubing, then use a crimp bead to connect the beading wire to half of the clasp, and then attach a crimp cover. Repeat to finish the other side of the necklace.

By Fernando DaSilva

Oh, Betsey

This piece features art nouveau lines while maintaining a fresh, edgy and provocative feel. I've taken my inspiration for this piece from the fabulous fashion designer Betsey Johnson. She has taken fashion to a unique aesthetic, creating clothes that are dramatic and vibrant yet approachable. I liken the spirit of her designs to the flair of Spanish flamenco dancers. In this spirit of exuberance, I chose the time-tested combination of pink and black. Rubber eyeglass holders form links between the beads and create an interesting texture. The center pendant is a pointed jet crystal that really steals the show.

Materials

1 40mm jet avant garde crystal pendant

4 18mm × 12mm black diamond crystal polygon beads

4 18mm jet large-hole crystal rondelles

1 6mm jet crystal bicone pendant

1 6mm rose crystal bicone pendant

1 6mm black diamond crystal bicone pendant

12 black eyeglass holders

4" (10cm) ⅜" (1cm) thick black velour tubing

1 spool 20-gauge pink Colourcraft wire

36" (91cm) 24-gauge silver-plated German-style wire

59 4mm copper jump rings

1 copper S-hook clasp

Tools

wire twister

jump ring maker

chain-nose pliers

round-nose pliers

nylon-jaw pliers

wire cutters

Betsey Ring

Attach several beads to a bling ring—an adjustable ring with several built-in loops. Use fuchsia, pink, rose and jet beads, as in the necklace. It is the perfect complement to your necklace and makes that Betsey Johnson statement with enough oomph to wear on its own. If you must wear earrings, simple hoops would do nicely. People will be stopping you on the street when you wear this ring!

ONE • Begin to create twisted-wire bail

Twist 2 18" (46cm) pieces of German-style silver-plated wire and 1 18" (46cm) piece of pink Colourcraft wire together very tightly, following the directions on the wire twister. Cut off the ends of the twisted wire and cut at least a 4" (10cm) piece to use for the bail, making certain there are no bumps or irregularities in the wire. Carefully bend ⅛" (3mm) of the end of the wire back against itself using chain-nose pliers. Begin turning the wire to form a coil. Make approximately 2½ revolutions around the original bend to make a small coil. Bend the wire in a 90-degree bend straight up, forming a large coiled head pin. Thread the coiled wire through the large pendant, but do not pull the inside bend of the coil flush with the front face. Leave enough distance for a wrap with the end of the wire.

TWO • Finish twisted-wire bail

Bend the wire up at a 90-degree angle at the back of the crystal pendant, then form an open bend about the thickness of the pendant and back down toward the inside edge of the front of the pendant. Wrap the wire around the base of the coil plus an additional 3-quarter turn. Trim the excess twisted wire. Bend a piece of twisted wire around the 8mm jump ring maker mandrel 3 times. Use flush cutters to cut the 3 wraps into large jump rings. Attach the jump ring to the pendant. (See Techniques, page 141, for instructions on opening and closing a jump ring.)

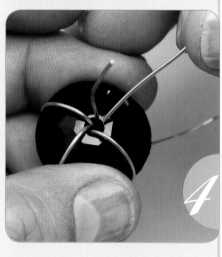
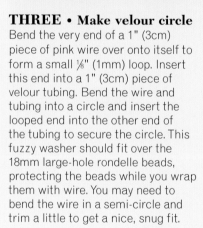

THREE • Make velour circle

Bend the very end of a 1" (3cm) piece of pink wire over onto itself to form a small ⅛" (1mm) loop. Insert this end into a 1" (3cm) piece of velour tubing. Bend the wire and tubing into a circle and insert the looped end into the other end of the tubing to secure the circle. This fuzzy washer should fit over the 18mm large-hole rondelle beads, protecting the beads while you wrap them with wire. You may need to bend the wire in a semi-circle and trim a little to get a nice, snug fit.

FOUR • Wrap rondelle with pink wire

Slip the velour tubing washer over an 18mm rondelle. Cut an 8" (20cm) piece of pink Colourcraft wire and insert it into the bead, leaving approximately 1½" (4cm) of wire at the top of the bead. Then carefully bend the wire back over the bead and the washer and insert the long end back into the top of the bead. Wrap the bead 4 times and adjust the wires so they're equidistant from each other. Remove the washer by separating it at the seam. Repeat this step with each of the rondelles.

Twist the wires until one or more breaks by itself. They usually break at the end so you will have plenty of useable twisted wire for the project. Remember—this is a more advanced project, so take your time.

tip

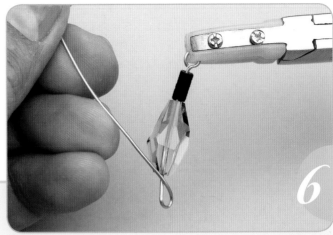

FIVE • Create wire twist

Grasp a wrapped rondelle with your fingers, making sure not to bend the wire loops. Grasp the midpoint of one of the wire loops with round-nose pliers and slowly twist the pliers in a clockwise motion until the wire bends into an S shape. This may take some practice, so don't panic. Make another clockwise twist in the wire on the opposite side of the bead. Repeat this step for all the wire loops on each of the rondelles. Make wrapped loops above and below each bead using round-nose pliers. (See Techniques, page 140, for instructions on making a wrapped loop.) Trim away the excess wire with flush cutters.

SIX • Begin to create beaded segmet

Cut a 7" (18cm) piece of pink Colourcraft wire. Turn a loop at 1 end. (See Techniques, page 140, for instructions on turning a loop.) Cut a ⅜" (1cm) piece of velour tubing lengthwise to use as a spacer. String the split velour tube onto the Colourcraft eye pin, then string on a 14mm polygon bead. Hold the loop with nylon-jaw pliers and bend the wire below the bead into a large loop. Bring the wire up and around the polygon in a swooping curve and wrap the tail around the base of the loop to secure the shape. Slip the spacer off the wire. Repeat this step for the remaining polygon beads.

SEVEN • Connect components with copper rings

Link components together with 2 copper jump rings in the following order: rondelle component, eyeglass holder, polygon component, eyeglass holder. Repeat this sequence twice. Then link a final eyeglass holder to the end of the necklace with a chain of 3 pairs of copper jump rings. Repeat to make the other side of the necklace.

EIGHT • Link beaded strands to pendant

Link the first eyeglass holder on each beaded strand to the twisted jump ring.

NINE • Attach clasp and dangle

Link the S clasp to 1 end of the necklace with a pair of jump rings. Link a chain of 6 pairs of jump rings to the other end of the necklace. Slide 3 top-drilled bicone pendants onto a final jump ring and link it to the final pair of jump rings in the chain.

By Margot Potter

Triptych

I have a three-dimensional brain, and I love working with hard wire because it allows me to create sculptural designs. These earrings are simple wire shapes tightly wrapped with thinner wire. I had to work with this idea and break more than a few beads until I came up with the final result, but I'm thrilled with how they turned out. Adding the incredibly reflective crystal vitrial rounds gives these funky earrings a touch of sophistication.

Materials

approximately 58–66 4mm crystal vitrial AB rounds

copper, bright blue and mint green 20-gauge Colourcraft wire

24-gauge silver-plated Colourcraft wire

Tools

round-nose pliers

chain-nose pliers

nylon-jaw pliers

wire cutters

bead mat

safety goggles

large-grit sandpaper or metal file

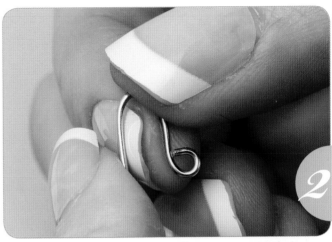

ONE • Begin to make wrapped shapes
Cut 2 3" (8cm) sections of 20-gauge wire in each of the following colors: copper, bright blue and mint green. Begin to make the shapes by forming a small loop at an end of 1 of the wire pieces with round-nose pliers.

TWO • Begin to coil wire
Use your fingers to bend the wire into a U shape in the opposite direction from the loop.

THREE • Coil wire
Grasp the wire with nylon-jaw pliers to keep the wire from getting nicked or marred. Loop the wire around to complete the coil. The coil should be about ½" (1cm) in diameter.

FOUR • Complete first coil
Trim the wire about ½" (1cm) above the coil, making sure to leave enough excess wire to make a bail. Bend the end of the wire up at a right angle. Grasp the wire at the bend with your round-nose pliers. Bend the wire over the pliers and around to form a rounded bail. Repeat to make another bright blue wire coil, spiraling the wire in the opposite direction to make a mirror image (to create a right and left earring). Make 2 copper coils and 2 mint green coils in the same manner, each in mirrored pairs, and each approximately ¾" (2cm) in diameter.

tip

When working with wire, run your hands along it periodically to keep it smooth. The heat of your hands prevents kinks.

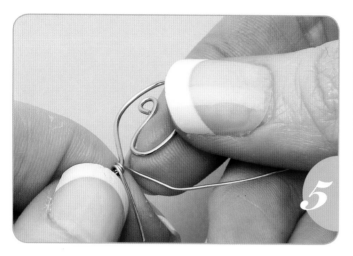

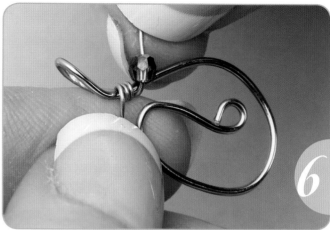

FIVE • Begin wrapping beads to wire shapes
Cut a 10" (25cm) section of 24-gauge wire. Beginning at the top of the first wire shape, wrap the wire around the thicker wire 4 times, leaving a small tail you can grasp while you start the coil.

SIX • Wrap on first crystal
String a crystal onto the wire, keeping it flush with the final wire wrap. Bring the wire around the blue wire, securing the crystal in place and keeping the crystal at the front of the shape. Continue wrapping crystals to the wire, approximately ⅛" (3mm) apart, adjusting the wires to keep the crystals to the front and maintaining enough tension that the beads remain in place. Work carefully and wear goggles in case a bead breaks. Continue wrapping your way around the shape until you almost reach the bottom loop. Wrap the thin wire around the core wire tightly 4 times. Trim away the excess wire and tuck the wire tail under with chain-nose pliers.

SEVEN • Wrap all shapes with crystals
Wrap each remaining shape with crystals and secure them with multiple wire wraps, as in step 6.

EIGHT • Link shapes together
Attach sections together by opening and closing bails around the bottom of each shape. The smaller blue coils should be on top, followed by the larger copper and mint green shapes.

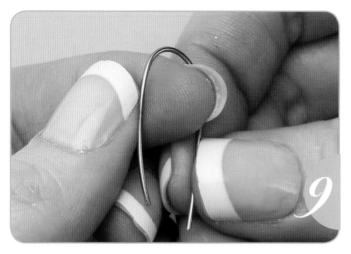
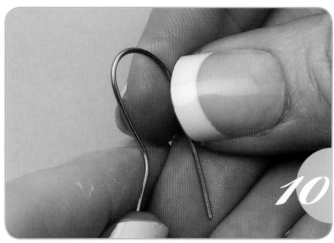

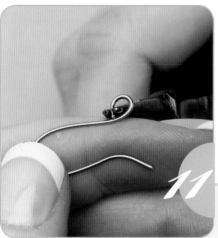

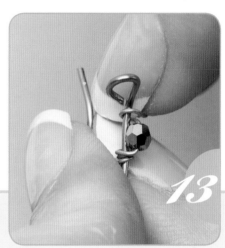

NINE • Shape ear wire
Cut 2 1½" (4cm) pieces of 20-gauge copper wire. Bend the center of 1 wire piece over your pointer finger.

TEN • Add slight bend to wire
Use your fingers or pliers to add a slight bend to 1 end of the wire.

ELEVEN • Loop end of ear wire
Use pliers to make a small loop on the other end of the ear wire.

TWELVE • Bend loop up
Grasp the loop with round-nose pliers and bend it up.

THIRTEEN • Add crystal to ear wire
Wrap a piece of thin 24-gauge wire around the front of the ear wire twice, then add a crystal and secure it by wrapping the wire around the core wire 2 more times. Cut the wire and tuck in the ends. Sand the wire ends lightly to smooth the wires. Link each set of 3 shapes to the ear wires.

4 Strange Strands

Designs Featuring Crinkle Wire, Multistrand Cable and Memory Wire

You'll never be stranded for great ideas once you've explored these ingenious designs. Wire is not just for simple stringing—this chapter is filled with projects that go beyond traditional beading. For example, watch how the simple switch from regular wire to Crinkle Wire totally transforms a waterfall-style exposed-wire design (see *Aurora*, page 84). Amazing! *Myth and Legend* (see page 82) combines Crinkle Wire and beads in a design that is positively striking! It looks complex, but it's quick to create and you'll be thrilled by the compliments you'll get when you wear it.

For a new twist on memory wire designs, check out the *Dazzle* choker (see page 90). Try using short memory wire segments with different colors and shapes for fun. Then take a walk on the futuristic side with the *Atmosphere* choker (see page 87) to learn a clever wire-wrapping technique. Good designers are restless and search endlessly for new materials and techniques. Be a design explorer and traverse uncharted territory—you'll discover all sorts of fantastic inspiration.

Create this chic, architectural choker with memory wire and double-hole sliders. Because the exposed wire is an integral part of the design, choose bright metallic wire instead of the dull stainless steel version. Vivid crystal colors will give the design extra pop.

By Katie Hacker

Architectura

Materials

4 6mm Indian red crystal rounds

3 6mm ruby crystal rounds

3 6mm purple velvet crystal helix beads

30 4.5mm simplicity black diamond crystal helix shape beads

108 4mm light gray crystal pearls

2 continuous 1½ loop sections of silver-plated necklace memory wire

11 silver double-strand spacer bars

4 5mm round silver memory wire end caps

Beadfix glue or epoxy

Structure Earrings

Use the structural look of the choker as your inspiration for these quick and easy earrings. Add purple velvet and violet opal crystals to head pins, and then make loops at the top of the head pins. The exposed wire mimics the architectural look of the choker and give the earrings extra swing!

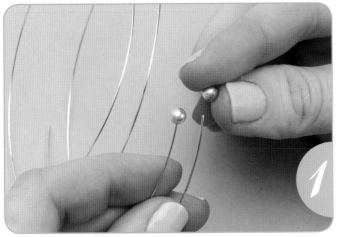

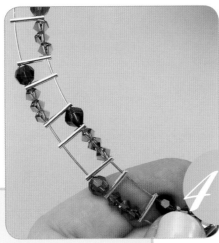

ONE • Glue on end caps
Glue a memory wire end cap onto 1 end of each piece of memory wire.

TWO • String on pearls and first spacer
String 27 pearls onto each wire. Pass the wires through the corresponding holes on a spacer bar.

THREE • String on first beaded sequence
Pass the upper wire through an Indian red crystal, then slide both wires through a spacer bar. String 3 black diamond crystals onto the upper wire, then slide both wires through another spacer bar.

FOUR • Continue beading necklace
Continue stringing on a 6mm bead followed by 3 black diamond beads, separating each grouping with a spacer. The 6mm beads follow this sequence: Indian red, ruby, purple velvet. Alternate between stringing beads onto the upper and lower wires so the crystals are staggered. Repeat the beading pattern until all of the black diamond crystals are used.

FIVE • Finish choker
Trim the memory wire ends to ⅜" (1cm) if necessary. Attach a memory wire end cap to each wire.

tip

It's easy to change the look of this choker. For a contemporary bridal look, use ivory pearls and crystal AB beads. If you prefer to make a choker with a clasp, substitute Beadalon stringing wire for memory wire.

By Margot Potter

Currents

When I was designing this piece, I was thinking about water—the fluidity of the Crinkle Wire creates what looks like a moving current to me. Beads float along the wire, suspended in the flow of the waving wire. The beads are simply loosely woven on six separate strands of wire, leaving interesting spaces between them that allow subtle movement.

Materials

1 18mm black diamond crystal twist bead

1 6mm white alabaster rondelle

4 11mm × 9mm crystal Galactic beads

5 8mm white alabaster crystal rounds

4 8mm black diamond crystal cubes

6 6mm mint alabaster crystal rondelles

6 6mm jet crystal rondelles

bright Crinkle Wire beading wire

4 5mm sterling jump rings

1 large silver-plated swivel lobster clasp

4 #4 silver-plated crimp tubes

4 sterling head pins

Tools

mighty-crimp tool

round-nose pliers

2 pairs chain-nose pliers

bead mat or board

wire cutters

Clear Currents

This same design done in clear crystal disco ball-style rounds looks completely different. I like the stark look of this in contrast to the more saturated original. Play! That's how great new ideas are born.

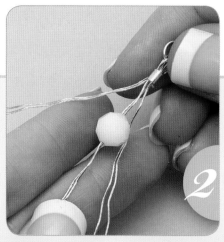

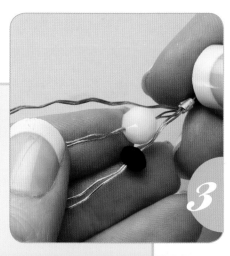

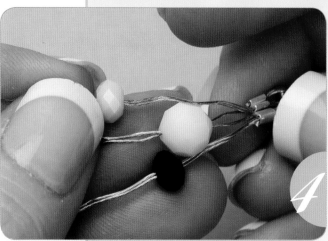

ONE • Crimp wire ends to jump ring
Cut 6 11" (28cm) strands of Crinkle Wire. Attach 3 strands to a jump ring with a single crimp tube, using pliers to pull the wires into the tube and leaving approximately ⅟₁₆" (2mm) of exposed wire at the jump ring to prevent wire wear. (See Techniques, page 138, for instructions on securing wire with a crimp tube.) Cut off the excess wire. Repeat with another set of 3 wires.

TWO • Thread on alabaster round
Thread a white alabaster round onto the center 2 wires.

THREE • Thread on jet briolette
Thread a jet rondelle onto the 2 outermost wires on the left side.

FOUR • Thread on mint alabaster briolette
Thread a mint alabaster rondelle onto the 2 outermost wires on the right side.

FIVE • Thread on Galactic bead
Thread a Galactic bead onto the 2 inside wires on the left side.

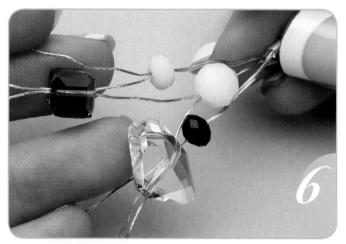

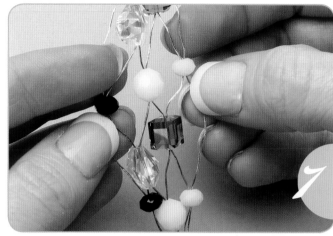

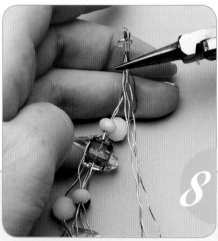

SIX • Thread on black diamond cube
Thread a black diamond cube onto the 2 inside wires on the right side.

SEVEN • Continue beading
Continue threading beads onto wire pairs in the established pattern until you've completed the sequence a total of 4 times. End the bracelet by threading an alabaster round, a black rondelle and a mint rondelle onto the pairs of wires as before. When you gently pull the wires apart, they'll look just like a fish net.

EIGHT • Crimp to secure design
Attach each set of 3 wire ends to a jump ring with a single crimp tube, using pliers to pull the wires into the tube and leaving approximately 1/16" (2mm) of exposed wire at the jump ring to prevent wire wear. Trim away any excess wire with wire cutters.

NINE • Create dangles
Slide the black diamond twist bead onto a head pin and make a wrapped loop above the bead. (See Techniques, page 140, for instructions on making a wrapped loop.) Also make dangles with a mint rondelle, an alabaster rondelle and a jet rondelle.

TEN • Add dangles and clasp
Attach a lobster clasp to 1 of the jump ring ends with a second jump ring. Add the dangles to the same jump ring end. (See Techniques, page 141, for instructions on opening and closing a jump ring.)

By Katie Hacker

Myth and Legend

I love fringy, dangly necklaces, and I'm always experimenting with ways to make designs that look like more than just beads on a string. Crinkle Wire lends great texture to these fringes, and the stainless steel color plays right into my color scheme. These colors remind me of those misty forest gatherings that you read about in books of myth and legend.

Tools

standard crimping pliers

chain-nose pliers

wire cutters

Materials

23 8mm erinite flat crystal briolettes

8 8mm erinite flat crystal briolettes

4 8mm palace green opal crystal rounds

25 6mm black diamond crystal rounds

31 4mm black diamond crystal rounds

51 4mm palace green opal crystal rounds

19 3mm silver sparkle round metal beads

1½ continuous loops of silver-plated necklace memory wire

.018" (.45mm) 7-strand bright crinkle wire

4 2mm clear oval Bead Bumpers

17 #2 silver crimp beads

34 #1 silver crimp tubes

2 3mm silver round memory wire end caps

Beadfix glue or epoxy

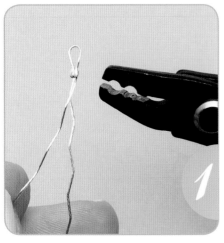

ONE • Begin to create fringe

Cut pieces of Crinkle Wire to the following lengths: 6 3" (8cm) pieces, 6 3½" (9cm) pieces, 2 5" (13cm) pieces, 1 3½" (9cm) piece, 1 4½" (11cm) piece, 1 6½" (17cm) piece. Pass both ends of 1 wire piece through a #2 crimp bead and slide the crimp up ¼" (6mm) from the fold. Crimp the bead in place with crimping pliers. (See Techniques, page 138, for instructions on using a crimp bead.) Repeat for each wire.

TWO • Add beads to fringe

String assorted crystals and sparkle beads onto the wire ends in different combinations of 3 or 4 for the short wires and groups of 6 or 8 for the longer wires. Use chain-nose pliers to flatten a crimp tube onto each wire end.

THREE • String fringe onto necklace

String the 3½" (9cm), 4½" (11cm) and 6½" (17cm) Crinkle Wire beaded fringe onto the center of the memory wire.

FOUR • String on beads and fringe

On 1 side of the central fringe, string on an 8mm palace green opal and a 5" (13cm) fringe. Alternate between beads and fringe in the following sequence: 8mm erinite briolette, fringe, 6mm black diamond, fringe, erinite briolette, fringe, palace green opal, fringe. String on the fringe from longest to shortest. Repeat the sequence once more, ending with the second erinite briolette. End the beaded section by stringing on a 3mm silver sparkle round metal bead and 3 4mm palace green opal rounds on each side.

FIVE • Finish pattern

Repeat the pattern on the other side of the necklace so it's symmetrical. Adjust the beaded section to center it on the memory wire.

SIX • String on bead bumpers

String 2 Bead Bumpers onto each side of the beaded section to hold it in place.

SEVEN • Glue on end caps

Glue memory wire end caps onto the wire ends.

By Fernando DaSilva

Aurora

As a designer, I am driven to imagine different ways to update one of the most common jewelry items: a chain. I am addicted to chain because it's easy to work with and provides endless possibilities. For this super sparkly necklace I've combined crinkle wire and diamond-shaped chain—they seem to be created for each other. The exciting combination of shapes and the dazzling effect of light produced by the sparkling tassel make this dramatic necklace a must-have.

Materials

12 10mm × 5.5mm navette set of crystal AB DIY items

6 8mm white alabaster crystal bicones

6 8mm light azore crystal rounds

18 6mm light gray opal top-drilled crystal bicone pendants

36 3mm AB satin crystal bicones

1 30mm moonlight crystal pendant

1 20mm tanzanite Galactic vertical crystal pendant

2' (61cm) .018" (.045mm) bright Crinkle Wire

3' (91cm) large silver-plated diamond-shaped chain

2' (61cm) small silver-plated diamond-shaped chain

1 silver-plated heavy oval jump ring

24 6mm silver-plated jump rings

3 4mm silver-plated jump rings

2 silver-plated 2-strand slide-bar clasps

1 large silver-plated EZ-Lobster Clasp

2 silver-plated pinch bails

24 silver-plated chain connectors

8 silver-plated EZ-Crimp ends

Tools

chain-nose pliers

micro-crimp tool

mighty-crimp tool

bead reamer

wire cutters

84

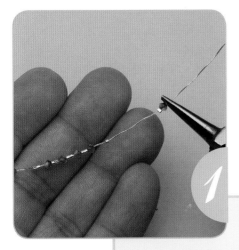

ONE • String crimp beads and crystals onto Crinkle Wire

Cut 6 5" (13cm) pieces of Crinkle Wire. String a crimp bead, an AB satin bicone and a crimp bead onto a 5" (13cm) piece of wire. Continue stringing on AB bicones sandwiched by crimp beads for a total of 6 bicones. Secure the beads in place between the crimp beads by flattening each crimp bead with chain-nose pliers. (See Techniques, page 138, for instructions on using a crimp bead.) Leave approximately ½" (1cm) at each end of the wire. Space the beads approximately ¼" (6mm) apart. Make a total of 6 beaded Crinkle Wire strands. Set them aside.

TWO • Enlarge EZ-Crimp end opening

Use the bead reamer to enlarge the hole of 1 EZ-Crimp end so it's large enough to accommodate 3 pieces of Crinkle Wire. Repeat for 1 more EZ-Crimp end.

THREE • Secure beaded wire strands in EZ-Crimp ends

Feed the ends of 3 beaded wires into the enlarged EZ-Crimp end and squeeze it with the mighty-crimp tool to secure the wires. Repeat for the remaining 3 wires and the remaining EZ-Crimp end with the enlarged hole.

FOUR • Attach beaded strands to slide-bar clasp

Attach 1 group of strands to each of the slide-bar clasp rings. Link an EZ-Crimp end to the free end of each strand.

FIVE • Link dangles to wire strands

Slide a light azore bead onto a head pin and turn a loop above the bead to make a dangle. (See Techniques, page 140, for instructions on turning a loop.) Make a second dangle with a white alabaster bicone. Open a 6mm jump ring and slide on 3 light gray crystal pendants. (See Techniques, page 141, for instructions on opening and closing a jump ring.) Link the azore dangle, the alabaster bicone dangle and the jump ring with the gray crystal pendants to the EZ-Crimp end on 1 of the Crinkle Wire strands. Repeat this step for the remaining strands.

Tassel Variation

Make an extra centerpiece using a slide clasp, a crystal moonlight pendant and a tanzanite Galactic pendant attached to the clasp with jump rings and pinch bails. Replace the original tassel with this pendant to give your creation a whole new look.

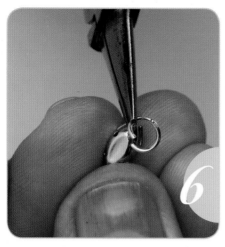

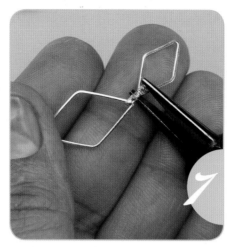

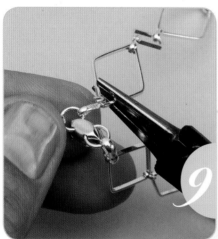

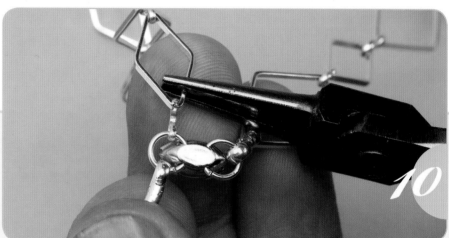

SIX • Create navette links
Link a 6mm jump ring to each side of each crystal navette. Create a total of 12 links.

SEVEN • Build diamond chain
Use chain-nose pliers to link a large diamond-shaped link to a small diamond link with a small silver-plated chain connector. Link another large diamond to the small diamond link with a small chain connector. Make 9 more of these large-small-large linked sections.

EIGHT • Link bar clasp to necklace center
Link a navette from step 6 to each of the loops on the bar clasp with a large chain connector. Link a diamond chain section to each of the navettes with a large chain connector. Link a navette to each diamond chain section, again using a large chain connector. Repeat once more on each side, ending with a navette.

NINE • Build center chain section
Link 4 diamond chain sections together with navettes. Link an end of this chain to the third navette up from the bar clasp with a large chain connector. Link the remaining free end of the diamond chain to the third navette up from the bar clasp on the other side of the necklace.

TEN • Connect inner chain to exterior chain
Separate 2 11-link sections of small diamond chain from the length of chain. Link an end of each section to either side of a navette. Link an end of this chain to the final navette in the core strand on either side of the necklace. Use a large connector to link a lobster clasp to 1 end of the necklace. Link a jump ring to the other end of the necklace with a final chain connector.

By Fernando DaSilva

Atmosphere

Sometimes the best inspiration comes when you open your eyes and see the stars. My inspiration for this project was drawn from the fantastic shape of CRYSTALLIZED – Swarovski Elements' Galactic crystal pendant and its facets. I visualized a futuristic design approach where the crystal is lifted high in a cage, like the rings of Saturn. Though my translation isn't exactly literal, the quick links from Beadalon allow me to make the edgy vision come true.

Tools

chain-nose pliers
round-nose pliers
memory wire shears
wire cutters

Materials

1 27mm tanzanite vertical Galactic crystal pendant

25 4mm tanzanite crystal cubes

26 4mm white alabaster satin crystal bicones

12 silver-plated solid rectangle rings

1¼ coils of silver-plated memory wire

3' (91cm) 24-gauge silver-plated German-style wire

1 20mm silver-plated round quick link

1 19mm × 41mm silver-plated oval Quick Link component

48 silver-plated double spacer beads

2 8mm silver-plated round twist jump rings

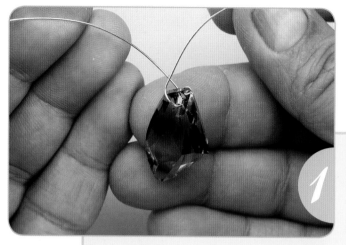

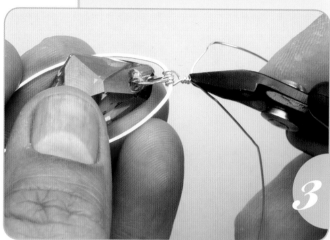

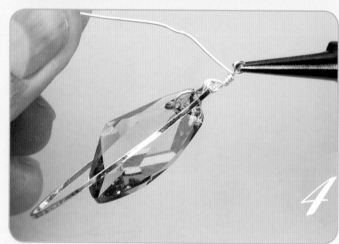

ONE • Thread wire through crystal pendant

Cut a 6" (15cm) piece of German-style wire, and bend it into a U shape. Slide the wire through the Galactic crystal pendant so the bottom of the U fits into the hole and the wire ends point up. Twist the wires together with 2 revolutions, making sure to allow the pendant to swing freely.

TWO • Twist wire to secure crystal inside oval

Separate the 2 wires enough to slide on the oval Quick Links solid ring. Wrap 1 wire over the solid ring 3 times, making the wraps as close together as possible. Repeat with the other wire end, securing the pendant to the oval ring.

THREE • Trim wrapping wire

Once the pendant is securely fastened to the oval ring, bend 1 of the wires straight up and wrap the other around the vertical wire twice. Use wire cutters to carefully cut the wrapping wire.

FOUR • Finish bail

Form a small loop in the remaining wire about ¼" (6mm) above the oval ring and wrap the end of the wire down the vertical wire until the wraps meet the previous wraps. Trim away any excess wire.

tip

It may take several attempts before you wrap the two links together just right. If you have not done any wire wrapping before, don't be frustrated. Just keep trying. German-style wire is not expensive, so cut off any failed attempts until you are satisfied with the wrapping.

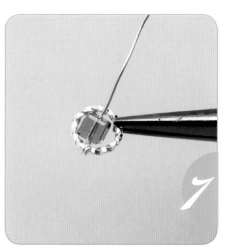
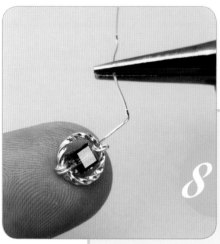
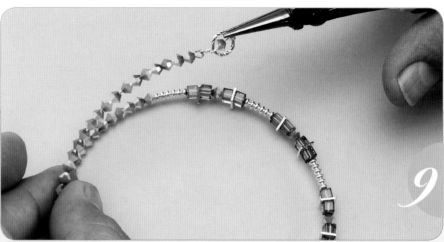

FIVE • Wrap second circle

Push the round ring onto the oval ring from the bottom to approximately a third of the way up (or as far as you can get it), making sure the Galactic pendant is inside the oval and the round ring. Cut 2 3" (8cm) pieces of German-style wire. Wrap 1 piece of the wire around the intersection of the Quick Links 3 times. Carefully cut the ends of the wires and tuck them inside of the newly made "cage." Repeat with the second wire at the other intersection, wrapping the wire in the opposite direction to create counter tension.

SIX • Bead center section of necklace

Using the memory wire shears, cut approximately 1¼ coils of necklace memory wire. String the pendant onto the memory wire, then string 3 double spacer beads onto the wire on both sides of the pendant. Continue stringing beads in the following sequence, beading the necklace symmetrically on each side: cube bead, solid rectangle ring, cube, bicone, cube, rectangle ring, cube, 3 double spacer beads. Repeat this pattern 2 more times, then string on 20 bicones.

SEVEN • Begin to create dangles for necklace ends

Cut a 2" (5cm) piece of German-style wire, and make a loop at 1 end with round-nose pliers. Thread the loop onto a twisted jump ring and close the jump ring. (See Techniques, page 141, for instructions on opening and closing a jump ring.) String a cube onto the wire.

EIGHT • Finish dangles

Wrap the end of the wire once around the opposite side of the twisted jump ring to secure the cube in the center of the ring. Create a loop at the top of the ring and wrap the wire around the base of the loop twice. Trim away any excess wire with flush cutters. Make another dangle with a bicone inside the jump ring.

NINE • Finish necklace

Using round-nose pliers, carefully turn a loop in each memory wire end just big enough to hold a dangle, making sure there is enough space for the beads to move freely and not be confined. (See Techniques, page 140, for instructions on turning a loop.) Link a dangle to each loop.

By Margot Potter

Dazzle

What if you took a memory wire bracelet and cut each circle in half? You'd have perfect half circles of tempered steel that would maintain their shape. Then what if you added EZ-Crimp ends to each wire half moon? You'd have wicked-cool curvy links to connect into organically-curved jewelry designs. I love the way the beads move along the wire and I love these enormous twist-crystal sew-on stones used as beads. This was a very fun design to create, and it's equally fun to wear.

Materials

4 28mm moonlight twist-crystal sew-on beads

15 12mm × 8mm silver crystal cubist beads

10 open-center silver-plated rectangles

5 ½-coil segments of bracelet memory wire

3 4mm silver-plated jump rings

1 small silver-plated toggle clasp

8 7mm × 9.5 silver-plated oval link rings

10 sterling EZ-Crimp ends

Tools

EZ-Crimp pliers

2 pairs chain-nose pliers

memory wire shears

90

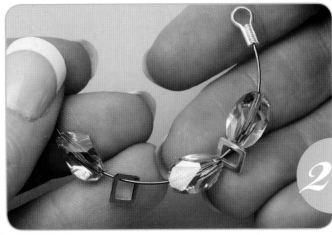

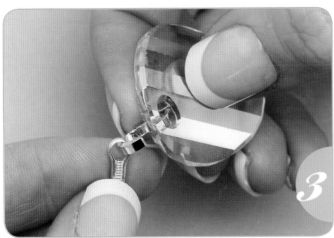

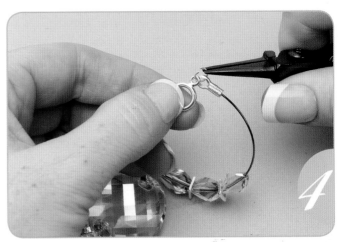

ONE • Secure EZ-Crimp ends to memory wire segments
Cut 5 ½-coil segments of bracelet memory wire (approximately 1¾" [5cm] wide when measured across both ends). Use memory wire shears only. Thread an end of a memory wire segment into an EZ-Crimp end and use the EZ-Crimp pliers to compress the end around the wire, securing it inside the crimp end. (See Techniques, page 139, for instructions on using an EZ-Crimp end.) Before securing the wire, be sure to face the opening of the EZ-Crimp end forward, as in the photo.

TWO • Thread beads onto wire segment
Thread the following beads onto the memory wire segment: cubist bead, open rectangle, cubist bead, rectangle, cubist bead. Secure the free end of the wire segment with another EZ-Crimp end. Repeat steps 1 and 2 to make a total of 5 beaded memory wire segments.

THREE • Link sew-on stones to beaded wire segments
Link a sew-on stone to a beaded wire segment with a metal link, compressing the link with your pliers. (Compressing the links with your pliers takes some effort.) Add a second sew-on stone to the opposite side of the beaded wire segment.

FOUR • Add toggle clasp
Link the next beaded segment to the free side of the sew-on stone with another metal link. Continue linking beaded wire segments to sew-on stones, ending with a beaded wire segment. Attach the bar end of a toggle clasp to 1 end of your necklace with a chain of 2 4mm jump rings. Attach the circle end of the toggle clasp to the opposite side with a single 4mm jump ring.

Supporting Players

Designs Featuring
Secondary Materials

It can be a challenge for a designer to expand his
or her vision and dream up new ways to use basic
jewelry components. In this chapter, we are bringing
design elements that usually play a secondary role
into the spotlight by transforming them into eye-
catching focal points. Toggle circles have become
sparkling links in the beautiful and sensuous
Connections necklace (see page 96) punctuated by
red CRYSTALLIZED – *Swarovski Elements* crystal
stones. Flower connectors take center stage in the
exotic, sparkly *Lakshmi* bracelet (see page 98).

Turn on the lights over your beading board,
get your tools and your crystals and join us on our
endeavor. You'll find that working with different
findings gives you an opportunity to stretch the inner
function of each finding and reinterpret the initial
purpose and reinvent it in a different way.

By Fernando DaSilva

Golden Glow

My mother never goes out in public without at least a pair of earrings. I know there are many women like her, and that led me to envision a pair of slim and elegant drop earrings suitable for many occasions. I realize they are a little long, but just imagine how daring and original you'll be when you adorn yourself with a little *Golden Glow*. In this design, I paired polished surfaces with rubber textures. The result, I think, is an updated version of the traditional drop earring. Combining the square CRYSTALLIZED – *Swarovski Elements* buttons with teardrop crystals and satin gold bead bumpers results in an edgy but wearable design.

Materials

2 24mm × 12mm Terrenum long crystal teardrop pendants

2 14mm light Colorado topaz square crystal buttons

24-gauge gold-plated German-style wire

14 4mm gold-plated light-weight jump rings

4 6mm gold-plated jump rings

2 gold-plated modern ear posts

4 gold-plated pinch bails

50 1.7mm satin gold cube Bead Bumpers

Tools

chain-nose pliers

round-nose pliers

mighty-crimp tool

wire cutters

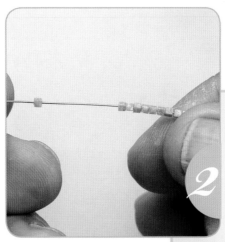

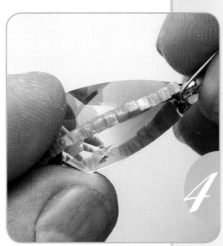

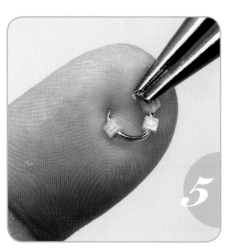

ONE • Add pinch bails to crystal beads

Slide a pinch bail into the hole in the long teardrop crystal. Squeeze the pinch bail closed using the outside jaw of the mighty-crimp tool. Use gentle pressure to avoid chipping the crystal. Secure 2 pinch bails to the square button, bringing each pinch bail through the center hole and again using gentle pressure with the mighty-crimp tool to secure the pinch bails closed.

TWO • String Bead Bumpers onto wire

String 25 satin gold Bead Bumpers onto approximately 4" (10cm) of silver German-style wire.

THREE • Wrap wire around bead

Bend the tip of 1 end of the wire strung with Bead Bumpers into an U shape. Slide the hooked wire onto the pinch bail and bend the end of the wire into a loop. (See Techniques, page 140, for instructions on turning a loop.) Trim away the excess wire tail with wire cutters. Wrap the Bead Bumpers vertically around the teardrop.

FOUR • Secure wire to pinch bail

Wrap the beaded wire completely around the teardrop and then tightly wrap the wire around the pinch bail several times to secure the strand. Trim away any excess wire.

FIVE • Slide Bead Bumpers onto jump ring

Open a 6mm round jump ring and string 4 Bead Bumpers onto it. Close the ring. (See Techniques, page 141, for instructions on opening and closing a jump ring.)

SIX • Link earring components

Link the teardrop to the square crystal with 2 4mm gold jump rings. Link the beaded jump ring to the top of the square with 2 more 4mm jump rings. Slide a single 4mm jump ring through the hole in the earring finding. Link the beaded jump ring to the earring finding with 2 final jump rings. Repeat steps 1–6 to make a second matching earring.

By Katie Hacker

Connections

Y-shaped necklaces like this one are a jewelry maker's staple because they're so versatile. The design naturally lends itself to a variety of interpretations. For this piece, I used a dramatic sew-on stone as my starting point. From there, I built the center of the necklace, then added the sides. Small toggle rings act as links and echo the geometric channel-set crystals.

Materials

1 18mm crystal sew-on stone

3 14mm crystal cosmic rings

5 8mm Siam round double-loop channel-set crystals

3 6mm clear round single-loop channel-set crystals

small silver curb chain

9 8mm round silver jump rings

17 4mm round silver jump rings

10 silver toggle rings

1 silver toggle clasp

Tools

chain-nose pliers

wire cutters

ONE • Link Siam channel to toggle

Thread a 4mm jump ring onto the loop of a circle toggle component and slide a Siam crystal channel onto the open ring. Close the ring, linking the toggle component to the channel. (See Techniques, page 141, for instructions on opening and closing a jump ring.) Link a second circle toggle component to the other loop on the channel with a second 4mm jump ring.

TWO • Link toggle to crystal circle

Link a cosmic ring to 1 of the toggle circles with an 8mm jump ring.

THREE • Finish core of necklace

Build a second toggle circle-and-channel-chain component as in step 1 and link it to the cosmic ring with another 8mm jump ring. Link an end of this chain to the sew-on stone with an 8mm jump ring. Build the second half of the necklace and link it to the same hole in the sew-on crystal with a second 8mm jump ring.

FOUR • Begin to build central tassel

Link a toggle circle to the bottom of the sew-on stone with an 8mm jump ring. Link a channel chain to this toggle with a 4mm jump ring. Link a cosmic ring to the channel with an 8mm jump ring. Link a toggle circle to the cosmic ring with another 8mm jump ring. Before closing the ring, slide on another circle toggle. Separate out a 2" (5cm) section of chain. Separate out 2 more short sections of chain, making the second section 2 links shorter than the first, and the third section 2 links shorter than the second, to create a staggered effect. Link a clear crystal channel to the end of each chain with a 4mm jump ring.

FIVE • Finish building central tassel

Slide all 3 chains from step 4 onto a 4mm jump ring and link this ring to the loop on the final circle toggle in the central tassel.

SIX • Link chains to toggle clasp

Separate out 6 4" (10cm) sections of chain. Use a 4mm jump ring to attach 3 of the chains to the toggle ring. Use another 4mm jump ring to attach the remaining 3 chains to the toggle bar. Link each grouping of 3 chains to a side of the necklace with 4mm jump rings.

By Fernando DaSilva

Lakshmi

This exotic-looking bracelet evokes Lakshmi, the Hindu goddess of wealth and riches. I love the opulence of high-karat jewelry and the craftsmanship it involves. I found a way to re-create it that doesn't require stone setting or soldering—and the result is still mind-blowing. Using simple jump rings and flower connectors you can now achieve that detailed and intricate look. Wear this bracelet and pose as a priestess ready to bestow your blessing upon the Western world.

Materials

2 14mm copper crystal cosmic pendants

4 11mm × 5.5mm copper crystal briolettes

16 4mm tourmaline crystal bicones

16 4mm olivine Dorado crystal bicones

16 3mm olivine AB crystal rounds

39 gold-plated 4-way flower connectors

68 3.5mm gold-plated lightweight jump rings

2 3.5mm × 4.5mm gold-plated oval jump rings

6 4mm gold-plated round jump rings

1 gold-plated hook-and-eye clasp

48 small gold-plated ball head pins

2 gold-plated 3-to-1 Victorian ring connectors

Tools

jump ring tool

standard crimping pliers

chain-nose pliers

round-nose pliers

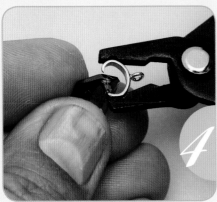

ONE • Begin to connect flowers
Using chain-nose pliers and the jump ring tool, open all the 3.5mm jump rings, pulling them open just enough to accept the ring on the flower connectors. Use the jump rings to link 13 flowers together.

TWO • Create 3 strands of connected flowers
Repeat step 1 to make a total of 3 strands of 13 linked flowers. Make sure to take the time to securely close each jump ring as fully as possible to ensure a really wonderful finish. Use 3.5mm jump rings to link all 3 strands together.

THREE • Connect gold strands to clasp
Link the end of each strand to the corresponding loop on a 3-to-1 connector. Repeat for the other end of the bracelet. Link each component of the clasp to an end of the bracelet with a single oval jump ring.

FOUR • Create large dangles
Slide a copper crystal cosmic pendant onto a pinch bail and squeeze the pinch bail closed with crimping pliers. Slide a 4mm jump ring onto the loop at the top of the pinch bail. Repeat with a second copper cosmic pendant. Slide each copper briolette onto a 4mm jump ring. Set these dangles aside.

FIVE • Link dangles to bracelet
Slide a tourmaline bicone onto a ball head pin and turn a loop above the bead. (See Techniques, page 140, for instructions on turning a loop.) Repeat to make dangles with all the tourmaline bicones and all the olivine rounds. Link 2 olivine dangles to each of the first 2 outside holes on both sides of the bracelet. Then link 2 tourmaline bicones to the next 4 outside holes on both sides of the bracelet. At the middle, slide a briolette, a cosmic pendant and another briolette onto the flower loop. Bead the second half of the bracelet in the same manner as the first.

Refer to this illustration for a close up of how the flowers are linked with jump rings.

Lakshmi Earrings

Connect flower links to two three-to-one Victorian connectors to create these chandelier-style earrings. Use the same beads and add one copper briolette in the center ring. Attach the components to lever-backs and experience your inner goddess.

When I saw these loose metal links, the idea to link them into an asymmetrical bib immediately popped into my brain. There was a fair amount of arranging and rearranging before I got the right combination of shapes, but I'm delighted with the way this design turned out. Instead of sparkly beads, I chose crystal pearls and white alabaster rounds for a more understated effect. This necklace is so effortlessly chic, and it's very easy to reproduce.

By Margot Potter

Curvilinear

Tools

round-nose pliers
2 pairs chain-nose pliers
wire cutters

Materials

9 8mm powder almond crystal pearls

9 8mm powder green crystal pearls

8 6mm white alabaster crystal rounds

4 1" (3cm) silver-plated oval Quick Links rings

5 ¾" (2cm) silver-plated circle Quick Links rings

1 1" (3cm) silver-plated circle Quick Links rings

1 11-link, 1 6-link alternating ovals Quick Links chain

26 5mm silver-plated jump rings

1 large silver-plated swivel lobster clasp

18 large Quick Links connectors

26 sterling silver or silver-plated head pins

Curvilinear Earrings

It's super easy to make a flirty pair of earrings by adding two of each beaded dangle to the bottom larger oval in a two-link section of chain. Remove the Quick Links connectors at the top and bottom and you've got your readymade earring component. Then just add an ear wire to the top, and you're done!

ONE • Arrange links for central bib

Arrange the center section of links on your work surface (a bead mat works well). From top to bottom as pictured, the links are: ¾" (2cm) circle link, 1" (3cm) oval link, 2 ¾" (2cm) circle links; oval link, ¾" (2cm) circle link, oval link; 1" (3cm) circle link, ¾" (2cm) circle link; oval link.

TWO • Begin linking ovals

Beginning with the lowest oval link, attach the links to each other with peanut-shaped connectors, using chain-nose pliers to close them.

THREE • Finish bib

Continue to build the design, working up and out as you go. Be sure to keep all of the connectors facing the same direction. Attach the shorter section of chain to the right top link on the bib (as it's facing you). Attach the longer section of chain to the left top link on the bib. Attach the lobster clasp to the end of the shorter section of chain.

FOUR • Link dangles to central pendant

Slide each bead onto a head pin and make a wrapped loop above each bead. (See Techniques, page 140, for instructions on making a wrapped loop.) Slide 1 of each kind of dangle onto 1 jump ring and set it aside. (See Techniques, page 141, for instructions on opening and closing a jump ring.) Slide each remaining dangle onto a jump ring. Slide 15 dangles onto the center bottom oval in the bib formation.

FIVE • Link dangles to necklace

Attach a single dangle to each of the larger oval links in the chain, working from the center out in the following pattern: green pearl, almond pearl, alabaster round. Attach a total of 3 dangles on the shorter side and 5 dangles on the longer side.

SIX • Link dangle to end of chain

Link the jump ring with 1 of each kind of bead from step 4 to the final link in the longer section of chain at the back of the necklace.

Fringe Elements
Designs Featuring Chain and Tassels

In this chapter, you'll find unique approaches to incorporating chain and tassels into your jewelry designs. Chain can be far more than just a basic background element. Make it the main event by combining several strands and hanging just a few large pendants (see *Moonstruck*, page 109). Or make your own chain by linking jump rings into a silvery net where crystal rings are ensnared, as in the *Lady of the Rings* necklace (see page 115).

And who says cones have to be strictly relegated to the behind-the-scenes work of keeping multiple strands bundled neatly together? Bring cones from the background into the spotlight by using them to create the metallic sparkly tassels in the *Cascade* earrings (see page 104). You'll also learn how to use cones to make a swinging central tassel in the *Evening Topaz* necklace (see page 106).

By Margot Potter

Cascade

I love how the exposed wire tendrils explode out of the cones in these earrings. This beaded wire fringe is a fun new take on a traditional idea. I wanted to make the colors festive, like a fireworks display. This was a more-the-merrier situation, because the more cones I made, the better the earrings became.

Tools

round-nose pliers

chain-nose pliers

wire cutters

Materials

10 4mm padparascha crystal rounds

10 4mm Indian sapphire crystal rounds

10 4mm light topaz crystal rounds

10 4mm black diamond AB crystal rounds

.018" (.45mm) Satin Gold wire

8 gold-plated cones

8 gold-plated eye pins

8 gold-plated head pins

8 gold-plated kidney ear wires

32 gold-plated crimp beads

4 5mm gold-plated jump rings

2 small gold-plated toggle circle ends

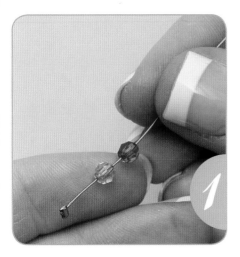

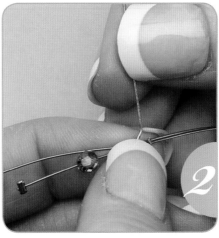

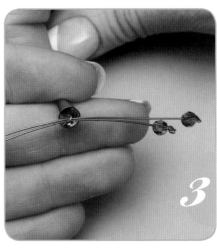

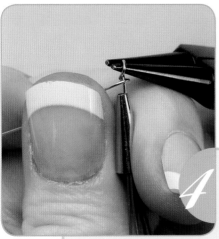

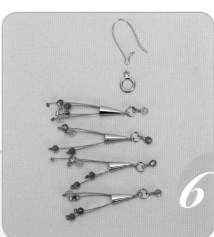

ONE • Thread beads onto wire
Cut 8 3" (8cm) segments and 8 2¾" (7cm) segments of Satin Gold wire. Flatten a crimp bead flush to the end of a wire section using chain-nose pliers. Slide a light topaz and a padparascha bead onto the wire. Flatten a crimp bead flush to the open end of the wire. Use wire cutters to cut off any excess wire. Repeat to make another beaded segment with an Indian sapphire and a black diamond bead. Repeat to make a total of 8 padparascha and light topaz beaded segments and 8 Indian sapphire and black diamond beaded segments.

TWO • Thread wires through eye pin
Thread 2 beaded segments, 1 padparascha-topaz and 1 sapphire-diamond, onto the pre-opened end of an eye pin.

THREE • Pull eye pin inside cone
Close the eye pin and thread it into a cone. Keep the wires even as you pull the tail of the eye pin inside the cone, using round-nose pliers to grab the wire.

FOUR • Make wrapped loop above cone
Keep tension on the eye pin as you create a coiled loop flush to the top of the cone. (See Techniques, page 140, for instructions on making a wrapped loop.) Repeat to make fringe with 4 cones for each earring, creating 2 cones for each earring with short tassels and 2 with long tassels.

FIVE • Create dangles
Slide each of the remaining beads (2 of each color) onto head pins and make a wrapped loop above each bead.

SIX • Link components together
Slide 1 dangle and 1 cone onto a jump ring. Repeat for the remaining cones and dangles. Link 4 jump rings together in a chain, then link the top jump ring to a toggle clasp ring. Link the ring to an ear wire. Repeat to make the second earring.

— *By Katie Hacker*

Evening Topaz

Cones are typically used at the ends of multiple-strand jewelry. But why hide them in the back? I decided to bring them front and center with this simple necklace design. They make great toppers for teardrop briolette beads and for easy chain tassels.

Tools

standard crimping pliers

chain-nose pliers

round-nose pliers

wire cutters

Materials

1 14mm crystal tabac round flatback crystal sew-on stone

1 10mm crystal dorado round flatback crystal sew-on stone

1 9mm × 6mm light Colorado topaz crystal teardrop briolette

1 8mm smoked topaz crystal round

1 6mm smoked topaz crystal round

1 4mm light Colorado topaz crystal round

1 3mm gold sparkle round metal bead

8mm gold filigree bead cap

4 12mm gold beading cones

gold-dapped small cable chain

22-gauge gold craft wire

1 5mm gold jump ring

gold swivel lobster clasp

3 gold ball-and-star head pins

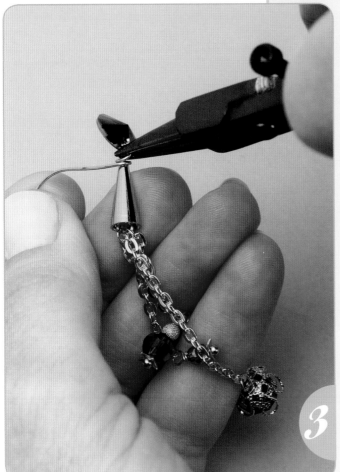

ONE • Begin to make tassel

Slide an 8mm smoked topaz crystal and a bead cap onto a head pin and turn a loop above the bead. Thread the loop onto the end of 1½" (4cm) piece of chain. Wrap the wire around the base of the loop to secure the bead to the chain. (See Techniques, page 140, for instructions on turning a loop and making a wrapped loop.)

TWO • Slide chains onto wire

Slide a 4mm smoked topaz crystal and a sparkle bead onto a head pin and link them to a 1¼" (3cm) piece of chain with a wrapped loop. Repeat with a 4mm light Colorado topaz crystal and a 1" (3cm) piece of chain. Cut a 3" (8cm) piece of craft wire and make a wrapped loop at 1 end. Slip the chain dangles onto the loop and wrap the wire around the base of the loop to secure the chains. Trim away any excess wire with wire cutters.

THREE • Finish tassel

Thread the wire into a beading cone, then make a wrapped loop flush with the top of the cone, slipping the 10mm sew-on stone onto the loop before wrapping it closed.

FOUR • Link sew-on stones

Use a jump ring to connect the 2 sew-on stones (See Techniques, page 141, for instructions on opening and closing a jump ring.)

FIVE • Link second cone

Cut a 3" (8cm) piece of craft wire and make a wrapped loop to attach it to the 14mm sew-on stone. Thread a briolette bead onto the wire, wide part first, and then slide on a beading cone, fitting the opening of the cone on top of the bead. Use the widest part of the round-nose pliers to make a large wrapped loop.

SIX • Link chains to clasp

Separate out 3 15" (38cm) chain sections and hold them together. String the pendant onto the center of the chains. Slide the ends of all 3 chains onto a 3" (8cm) piece of wire and make a wrapped loop. Slide a beading cone onto the wire and make another wrapped loop above the cone, attaching the clasp before wrapping the loop closed. Repeat to finish the other end of the necklace, making a large wrapped loop above the cone for the clasp to fasten onto.

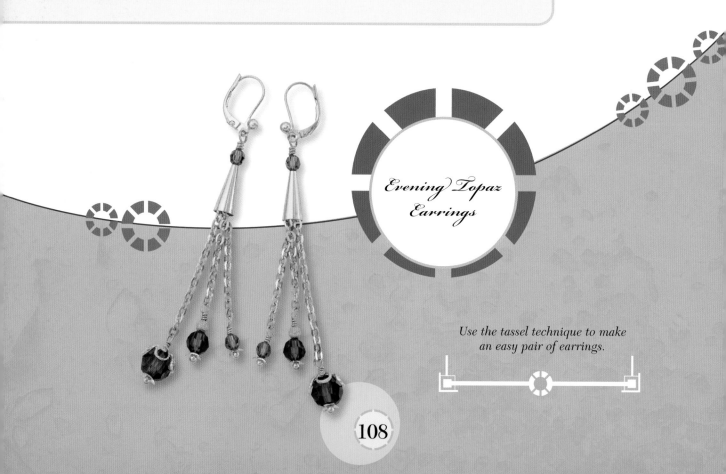

Evening Topaz Earrings

Use the tassel technique to make an easy pair of earrings.

By Margot Potter

Moonstruck

What if you made a Native American-style fitted choker and instead of strands of beads and sinew, you used chains? You'd have something that looks a bit like this necklace. Add bold, funky pendants to the bottom chain, and you are ready to rock and roll. This was an experiment in materials, and I like the way it turned out.

Materials

1 20mm crystal avant garde pendant

1 30mm crystal moon pendant

2 20mm metallic silver crystal crosses

6 6mm jet crystal briolettes

3 6mm crystal silver shade rounds

silver-plated rolo chain

silver-plated elongated cable chain

5 4-hole silver-plated spacer bars

22 5mm jump rings

8 3mm jump rings

4 large silver-plated swivel lobster clasps

20 silver-plated eye pins

9 sterling ball-tipped head pins

3 silver-plated pinch bails

Tools

2 pairs chain-nose pliers

round-nose pliers

mighty-crimp tool

wire cutters

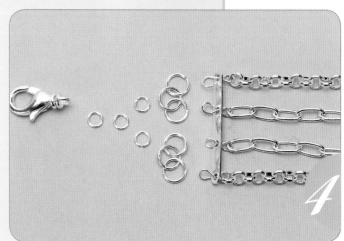

ONE • Separate chain

Separate the silver-plated rolo chain into 3 3-link sections and 3 25-link sections, using 2 pairs of chain-nose pliers to open and close the links. Separate the silver-plated elongated cable chain into 1 15-link section, 3 13-link sections and 3 12-link sections of silver-plated elongated cable chain, again using pliers. Set all the chains aside.

TWO • Prepare spacer bars

Thread an eye pin through the bottom hole of a spacer bar. Trim the wire to approximately ⅜" (1cm) and loop the wire end using round-nose pliers, bending the loop flush with the spacer bar. Repeat this process for every hole in every spacer bar to create the S-loops to which your chains will connect.

THREE • Link chains to spacer bars

Begin attaching chains to the spacer bars, working from top to bottom. Work section by section from top to bottom in the following order: 25-link rolo chain on the top rows, 12-link elongated chain on the second rows, 13-link elongated chain on the third rows, and 31-link rolo chain on the bottom rows. (The rows of chain are graduated to accommodate your neck. You can adjust the lengths of the chain to fit you, and there's also an extension chain for adjustments.)

FOUR • Link lobster clasp to necklace with jump ring chain

Create 2 jump ring chains of 3 rings each. Link the outer 2 jump rings in each chain to the top 2 and bottom 2 spacer bar loops, respectively. Link a smaller ring to the center ring of each 3-ring chain. Link both of these smaller jump rings to another small jump ring. Link the lobster clasp to the chain of jump rings with a final small jump ring. Repeat to build a jump ring chain on the other side of the necklace, but leave off the lobster clasp.

FIVE • Attach extension chain

Attach a 15-link section of elongated cable chain to the jump ring on the right side of the design to create an extension chain. Attach the avant garde pendant to the end of the chain with a 5mm jump ring.

SIX • Link jump rings to bottom spacer bars

Link a jump ring to the bottom or each spacer bar. There should be a total of 3 jump rings. You will attach beaded pendants to these later.

SEVEN • Create dangles

Slide a pendant onto a pinch bail and squeeze it closed with a mighty-crimp tool. Repeat for all 3 large beads.

EIGHT • Create decorative dangle

Create coiled dangles with the remaining beads. Slide the large moon pendant and crystal silver and jet briolette dangles onto a 5mm jump ring. Attach your beaded moon to a swivel lobster clasp on the beaded jump ring. Make a variety of pendants you can mix and match on the necklace as desired.

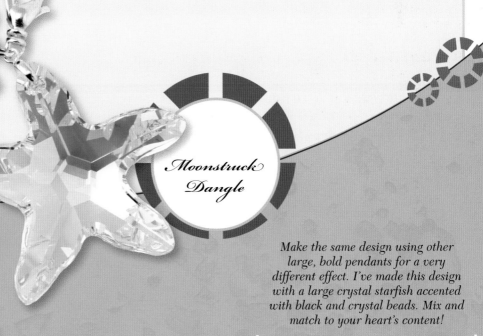

Moonstruck Dangle

Make the same design using other large, bold pendants for a very different effect. I've made this design with a large crystal starfish accented with black and crystal beads. Mix and match to your heart's content!

— By Margot Potter

Interlude

An unexpected combination of colors inspired by a dress on a catalog cover led me to make this very vintage-looking necklace. The Indian sapphire was my addition to the color pool. I'm influenced greatly by all things vintage, and I have a particular love of the work of Miriam Haskell. Her celluloid chain-and-charm necklaces inspired the vibe of this design. I bent the prongs on some lacy bead caps and put a smaller crystal in the center with a head pin to create flowers. From there I used chain sections as charms and added a variety of crystals to the front fabric chain section. The sleek triangle chain lent itself perfectly to the design, and a pretty extension chain with more flower dangles added just the right finishing touch.

Materials

7 12mm × 8mm crystal silver shade cubist beads

8 8mm light topaz crystal rounds

8 8mm Indian sapphire crystal rounds

7 8mm white alabaster crystal rounds

7 8mm crystal silver shade crystal rounds

7 6mm white alabaster crystal briolettes

5 6mm gray opal crystal briolettes

21 silver-plated filigree bead caps

gray fabric chain

silver-plated diamond chain

elongated cable chain

9 small open-oval silver-plated Quick Links rings

6 small open-square silver-plated Quick Links rings

33 5mm silver-plated jump rings

sterling silver lobster clasp

4 ball-tip sterling head pins

23 sterling head pins

18 silver-plated head pins

Tools

chain-nose pliers

round-nose pliers

wire cutters

ONE • Prepare chain

Remove 2 7-link sections of diamond chain. Remove a 17-link section of elongated cable chain. Cut a 33-link section of gray fabric chain. Arrange the chains on your work surface so you can see how they'll look when they're linked with jump rings.

TWO • Create flower dangles

Slide a bead cap followed by a crystal round onto a silver-plated head pin. Turn a loop above the bead to create a dangle. (See Techniques, page 140, for instructions on turning a loop.) Create a flower dangle with each crystal round for a total of 7 white alabaster flowers, 7 crystal silver flowers, 4 light topaz flowers and 3 Indian sapphire flowers.

THREE • Bend petals

Use chain-nose pliers to bend up alternating petals on each of the flower dangles.

FOUR • Slide flower dangles onto jump ring

Slide 3 flower dangles onto a single jump ring: light topaz flower dangle, alabaster and crystal silver. (See Techniques, page 141, for instructions on opening and closing a jump ring.) Make 3 more dangles with this grouping of flower dangles. Make 3 dangles with the following combination of flower dangles: Indian sapphire, alabaster and crystal silver.

Interlude Earrings

To make a matching pair of swingy little earrings, simply attach a light topaz flower cluster to a Quick Links diamond component with a jump ring, turning the light topaz flower to the front of the cluster before attaching the dangle. Slide the top of the diamond into the bottom of a lever-back earring component. Change the colors or the size of the beads and dangles to create an entirely different look.

113

FIVE • Create jump ring dangles
Slide each of the remaining crystal beads onto head pins and create a wrapped loop above each bead. (See Techniques, page 140, for instructions on creating a wrapped loop.) Make a total of 27 dangles: 5 gray opal, 7 white alabaster briolette, 7 cubist bead, 4 light topaz beads (2 on ball-tip and 2 on plain head pins) and 4 Indian sapphire (2 on ball-tip and 2 on plain head pins). Slide groupings of 4 and 3 dangles onto jump rings: 3 jump ring dangles with cubist bead, gray opal, light topaz and white alabaster; 2 jump ring dangles with cubist bead, gray opal and white alabaster. Also slide 3 links each of the oval and square Quick Links components onto jump rings for a total of 4 chain dangles.

SIX • Link dangles to fabric chain
Link dangles to the fabric chain from left to right in the following sequence, beginning at the second link and skipping 1 link between each dangle: sapphire, alabaster, crystal silver flower dangle; oval Quick Links dangle; cubist, white alabaster, gray opal jump ring dangle; ball-tip blue topaz round; light topaz, alabaster and crystal silver flower dangle; square Quick Links dangle; cubist, alabaster, gray opal and ball-tip light topaz jump ring dangle. Continue linking dangles to the fabric chain in this pattern, alternating between Indian sapphire and blue topaz in each floral and beaded cluster as you work.

SEVEN • Link fabric chain to metal chain
Link a 7-link section of diamond chain to an end of the beaded fabric chain with a 5mm jump ring. Link a second 7-link section of diamond chain to the other end of the fabric chain section. Add a 4-bead jump-ring dangle (from step 5) to the front of each jump ring.

EIGHT • Attach dangle to end of chain
Attach the lobster clasp with a jump ring to 1 end on the the metal chain. Attach the elongated cable chain with a jump ring to the other metal chain. Add the final linked floral cluster (featuring a light topaz bead) to the bottom of the cable chain with a jump ring.

114

By Fernando DaSilva

Lady of the Rings

This chain maille necklace is inspired by the strong female characters in *The Lord of The Rings*, especially Eowyn, who fought bravely against evil. She represents the archetype of a powerful and faithful woman who fights side by side with men. Beware, this project requires intensive work—but when you're finished, you'll see that the prize is totally worthy.

Materials

3 20mm crystal Tabac-foiled cosmic rings

11 20mm crystal silver shade column pendants

3 14mm crystal Tabac-foiled cosmic rings

440 6mm silver-plated jump rings

162 7mm × 9.5mm silver-plated solid oval rings

11 3.5mm × 4.5mm silver-plated oval jump rings

8 9mm silver-plated jump rings

1 silver-plated swivel badge clip

Tools

jump ring tool (optional)

2 pairs chain-nose pliers

bead mat or board

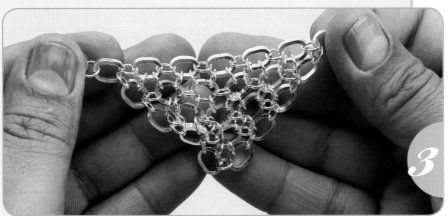

ONE • Make first chain

Start by opening a big pile of 6mm jump rings and set them aside.
(See Techniques, page 141, for instructions on opening and closing
a jump ring.) Link solid oval rings with 6mm jump rings, using 2
pairs of chain-nose pliers or a jump ring tool to ensure the rings
are closed correctly. Link 20 oval rings together to make the first
strand. Then link 1 final oval ring to the end of the 20-link chain
with 3 jump rings. Link 3 more jump rings to the other side of this
same final link.

TWO • Finish making chains

Make 4 more individual chains linking solid oval rings with 6mm
jump rings: 17-link chain, 16-link chain, 15-link chain, 14-link chain.
To get an overview of the design before you continue, align all 5
strands horizontally on your bead mat. Repeat steps 1 and 2 to
prepare the individual chains for the other half of the necklace.

THREE • Link chains together

Slide a jump ring onto the third solid oval ring from the end on
the longest individual chain. Link the first solid oval in the second
chain to this first oval. Close the ring. Slide another jump ring
onto the fourth solid oval ring from the end on the longest chain.
Use the jump ring to link this fourth oval to the first oval on the
second chain, and close the ring so the first link on the second
chain hangs between the third and fourth links on the first chain.
Continue connecting the first and second strands in this manner
so the links on the second chain are staggered between the links
on the first chain. Once the first 2 chains are linked, connect the
third, fourth and fifth chains in the same manner. Repeat for the
other side of the necklace. Now take a break! Your chain will look
like the picture above as you work.

FOUR • Attach dangles

Connect the second side of the necklace by linking the final oval ring in the top longest chain to the oval link with 3 jump rings from step 2. This is the center of your neckpiece. Carefully open a small oval jump ring and thread a crystal column pendant through its hole. Close it gently and then set it aside. Repeat with the remaining crystal pendants. Attach each of the 11 crystal silver shade column pendants to each of the 11 oval solid rings in the bottom front of the necklace with 2 jump rings together.

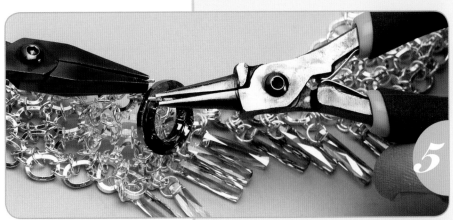

FIVE • Attach crystal rings

Open a 9mm jump ring enough to fit over a 20mm crystal Tabac cosmic ring, and close it carefully. Add a second jump ring; then set the ring aside to be attached in step 6. Repeat for all of the cosmic rings, using 6mm jump rings for the 14mm cosmic rings. Attach the cosmic rings to the neckpiece by opening and closing the 2 jump rings and linking them to any of the rings within reach. You may follow the placement as pictured, or create your own according to your preference. Remember to keep 2 larger and 1 smaller cosmic ring on 1 side and 1 larger ring and 2 smaller rings on the opposite side.

SIX • Attach clasp

Link the swivel badge clip to an end of the necklace with 3 6mm jump rings together. Link a 20mm cosmic ring to the other end of the necklace with 2 9mm jump rings together. Fasten the necklace by clipping the swivel badge clip to the cosmic ring.

Unusual Suspects
Designs Featuring Tubing, Leather, Silk and Thread

What is it that makes jewelry stand out in a crowd?
Is it the color? Is it the shape? Is it the design itself?
Outstanding jewelry designs are remarkable for all of
these reasons—and they stand out particularly well when
they're created with unexpected materials. Many of the
most intriguing designs are built around elements that are
not "typical" jewelry materials, such as tubing, cording
and leather. All the pieces in this chapter incorporate
an unusual element, but in an elegant way—the overall
impression is not focused on the material itself, but rather
on the beautiful effect of the creation as a whole.

In the *Woven Rings* necklace (see page 126), double
strands of leather weave in and out of twisted metal
rings creating an effect that's both subtle and bold—the
leather blends into the background of the design while
simultaneously creating the strong color palette. Velour
tubing creates vibrant waves in *Velveteen* (see page 124).
The *In Spades* necklace (see page 131) takes a fresh look
at the classic black-and-white color palette, where two
different sizes of tubing material hold clusters of milky
crystal beads. Perfect for day or evening, the *Neopolitan*
necklace (see page 122) and the *Zephyr* lariat (see page
120) are quick to make and fun to wear.
As you look through the pieces in this chapter, you
may just find that these unorthodox combinations of
unexpected elements with traditional beads and findings
will open up a whole new world of jewelry design.

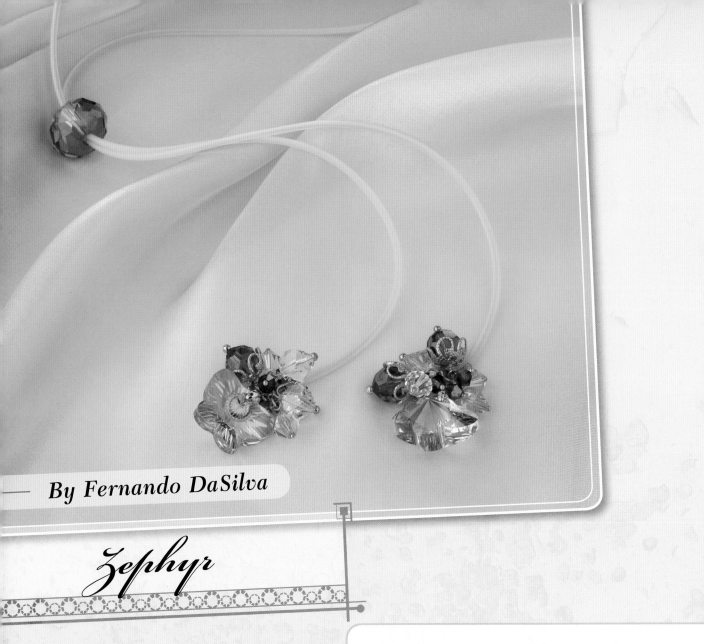

By Fernando DaSilva

Zephyr

I am a long-necklace fanatic. I am intrigued by the really serious ones, but I love the casual ones, too—they're fashion-forward and they embody youth! Long lariats are fun and evoke a certain old Hollywood glamour. In this version, I covered metallic wire with a frosted rubber cord, creating a fresh, high–tech veneer. Consider wearing this piece with a backless dress—size it tight around your neck like a choker and flip the dangles down your back. Or wear it with the dangles in front to dress up a casual top.

Materials

1 18mm copper large-hole rondelle bead

2 18mm crystal silver shade butterfly pendants

9 4mm Indian red crystal bicones

3 8mm Indian red AB crystal rounds

3 8mm silk crystal Helix beads

5 6mm light peach crystal bicones

28" (71cm) frosted rubber tubing

30" (76cm) .024" (.61mm) 49-strand 24K gold-plated stringing wire

20 1.5mm clear Bead Bumpers

6 gold-plated large ball head pins

14 gold-plated small ball head pins

2 gold-plated EZ-Crimp ends

2 gold-plated pinch bails

3 10mm gold-plated bead caps

8 3.5mm × 4.5mm gold-plated oval jump rings

Tools

chain-nose pliers

round-nose pliers

crimping pliers

EZ-Crimp pliers

wire cutters

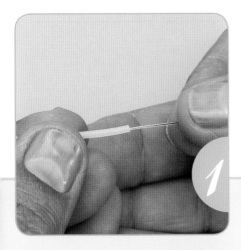

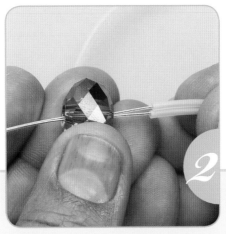

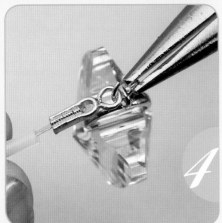

ONE • Insert wire into tubing

Insert approximately 17" (43cm) of gold stringing wire into a 15" (38cm) length of frosted tubing.

TWO • Pass tubing through copper bead

Double the covered tube and thread the 2 ends of the covered wire through an 18mm copper large-hole rondelle bead. Slide the bead up the tube-covered wire. Insert an end of the 24K gold-plated stringing wire into an EZ-Crimp end and squeeze it closed with EZ-Crimp pliers. (See Techniques, page 139, for instructions on crimping with the EZ-Crimp end.) Trim away any excess wire with wire cutters. Repeat for the other end of the wire.

THREE • Make butterfly dangle

Slide an 18mm butterfly pendant onto a pinch bail and use a crimp tool to carefully close the sides into the holes of the butterfly, closing the pinch bail as far as possible without chipping the sides of the pendant. Repeat to make a second butterfly dangle.

FOUR • Link butterfly dangle to crimp end

Link the butterfly pendant to an end of the lariat with a jump ring. (See Techniques, page 141, for instructions on opening and closing a jump ring.) Repeat for the other end of the necklace.

FIVE • Create and attach remaining dangles

Thread each round bead onto a large ball head pin followed by a bead cap and a clear Bead Bumper. Turn a loop above the beads or make wrapped loops, depending on your preference. (See Techniques, page 140, for instructions on turning a loop and making a wrapped loop.) Link 1 of these dangles to each crimp end. Thread each of the Helix beads onto head pins followed by Bead Bumpers and turn a loop above each bead. Thread each remaining bicone bead onto small ball head pins. Thread a Bead Bumper onto each head pin and make each into a dangle. Separate all the dangles into 4 random groupings and thread each grouping onto a jump ring. Link 2 groupings to each crimp end.

Do you prefer silver? Just replace the gold stringing wire with silver. Add turquoise AB and jet bead dangles and crystal butterfly pendants for a stunning casual urban look. This project is so easy, why not make both?

Blue Zephyr

— **By Margot Potter**

Neopolitan

For this necklace, I chose a color palette of pink, brown and gray—very retro colors that are currently back in vogue. I'm endlessly drawn to the beaded circle idea, and this version combines exposed bits of silk and metal with the beaded circles to create something of a crazy-quilt effect. I like using things like silk in unexpected ways, so instead of knotting the thread, I've tied off the ends and unraveled them. As soon as I finished this bracelet, I immediately thought of Neopolitan ice cream. Maybe that was my unconscious inspiration. Ice cream is always inspiring…isn't it?!

Materials

1 20mm crystal AB column pendant

57 4mm light smoked topaz crystal rounds

28 4mm crystal silver shade rounds

23 4mm rose water crystal opals

66 3mm light rose AB crystal rounds

2 1¼" (3cm) diamond-cuts silver-plated Quick Links rings

2 1" (3cm) squiggly silver-plated Quick Links rings

1 ¾" (2cm) diamond-cut silver-plated Quick Links heart

1 ¾" (2cm) diamond-cut silver-plated Quick Links square

1 1½" (4cm) silver-plated Quick Links oval

.018" (.45mm) 49-strand bright wire

#2 pink silk thread

#4 brown silk thread

3 5mm silver-plated jump rings

2 3mm silver-plated jump rings

silver crimp beads

1 small silver-plated toggle clasp

Tools

2 pairs chain-nose pliers

standard crimping pliers

scissors

jeweler's glue

wire cutters

tape

ONE • Wrap thread around circle link

Wrap brown silk around a large diamond-cut open-center circle so the link looks like it's been whip stitched along the edges.

TWO • Secure thread ends

Tie off the silk using an overhand knot followed by a surgeon's knot. (See Techniques, page 141, for instructions on tying a surgeon's knot.) Dab glue onto the knot and allow it to dry. Repeat the process to wrap pink silk around a large diamond-cut circle and a small squiggly Quick Links ring.

THREE • Create beaded circle

Cut a 3" (8cm) wire section and tape the end. Thread 16 3mm light rose and 11 4mm crystal silver rounds onto the wire. Thread the beaded wire through the silk-wrapped open circle and through a large oval Quick Links component (this oval link becomes 1 end of the necklace). Thread both ends of the wire into a crimp bead in opposite directions, creating a circle. Use crimping pliers to flatten the crimp bead. Cut away the excess wire.

FOUR • Continue linking necklace components

Link a circle beaded with 16 rose water crystal opal rounds to the brown-silk-wrapped link. Continue linking components in the following order: diamond-cut square; beaded circle alternating between 2 light smoked topaz and 1 rose AB crystal for a total of 24 beads; pink silk-wrapped circle; beaded circle of 28 rose AB crystals; beaded circle of 22 light topaz; heart link; beaded circle of 12 crystal shade rounds; squiggly circle; beaded circle with sequence of silver shade, light rose, rose water opal, light topaz repeating a total of 7 times; oval link; beaded circle alternating between 3 rose AB and 3 crystal shade for a total of 18 beads; pink silk-wrapped circle.

FIVE • Add knotted thread accents

Add small accent ties of brown or pink silk to the crimp-bead area of some (or all) of your beaded rings and dab glue on the knots so they will stay secured. Use your fingers to fray the ends of the thread once the glue has dried.

SIX • Finish neckace

Attach the toggle clasp to the necklace, using a 5mm jump ring for the toggle circle and a 5mm jump ring attached to 2 3mm jump rings for the toggle bar. (See Techniques, page 141, for instructions on opening and closing a jump ring.) Add the column pendant on a 5mm jump ring on the toggle circle clasp end.

By Katie Hacker

Velveteen

After I made the *Classic Combination* bracelet (see page 50), I was hooked on scallops! I wanted to see what would happen if I made the scallops bigger. After some experimentation, I realized that a single wire running through the entire design would create a dynamic look. The velour tubing makes the scallops trendy instead of precious.

Materials

12 8mm light Colorado topaz crystal flat briolettes

125 6mm smoked topaz crystal rounds

.018" (.45mm) 19-strand satin copper beading wire

brown velour tubing

2-strand silver slide clasp

4 #1 copper crimp beads

4 4mm copper crimp covers

adhesive tape or stopper beads

Tools

standard crimping pliers

mighty-crimp tool

wire cutters

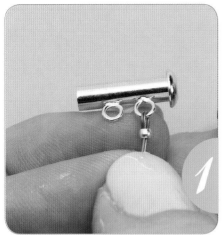

ONE • Crimp wire to clasp

Cut 2 36" (91cm) and 1 26" (66cm) length of beading wire. Cut 11 2" (5cm) pieces of velour tubing. Holding a 36" (91cm) and a 26" (66cm) length of wire together, secure them to a loop on the clasp with a crimp bead, using standard crimping pliers to attach the bead. Place a crimp cover over the crimp bead and use a mighty-crimp tool to close it. (See Techniques, page 138, for instructions on using crimp tubes and covers.) Repeat to attach the remaining 36" (91cm) wire to the other loop on the same half of the clasp.

TWO • Thread on first beaded sequence

Hold the set of 2 wires together and pass them through a smoked topaz and a light Colorado topaz bead. Pass the other wire through a smoked topaz bead and through the opposite side of the light Coloradao topaz bead. Drop the 26" (66cm) wire.

THREE • Thread on next beaded sequence

Pass each working wire through a smoked topaz bead, then pass the wires through opposite ends of another smoked topaz bead. Repeat this step twice more.

FOUR • Continue beading

Pass each working wire through a smoked topaz bead, then pass the wires through opposite sides of a light Colorado topaz bead. Repeat 10 more times. Pass each working wire through a smoked topaz bead and tape the ends of the wire or string on a stopper beads.

FIVE • String on first scallop

Pick up the empty wire near the beginning of the necklace and string on a piece of velour tubing.

SIX • Continue stringing scallops

Bring the wire through the next light Colorado topaz bead, then string on another piece of velour tubing. Continue making scallops in this same manner until you have a total of 11 scallops. Pass the wire end through the corresponding last smoked topaz bead. Attach the wire ends to the clasp as in step 1, again covering the crimp beads with crimp covers.

This fabulous, versatile necklace is created with an easy weaving technique. The suede lace and silver rings combine for a look that's stylish and comfortable to wear. Plus, you can easily change the design just by using a different pendant.

By Katie Hacker

Woven Rings

Green Woven Rings

Materials

1 28mm crystal round twist crystal pendant

1 6mm clear crystal channel

22 12mm silver twisted solid rings

blue faux suede lace

1 silver toggle clasp

2 silver fold-over crimps

2 4mm silver jump rings

1 6mm silver jump ring

1 8mm silver jump ring

Tools

scissors

chain-nose pliers

Here's an elegant twist on the same rings idea. Removing one strand of faux suede lace and adding lengths of chain with olivine beaded drops creates a more delicate effect that's suitable for evening.

ONE • Weave suede lace through rings
Cut 2 16" (41cm) pieces of suede lace. Place 2 twisted rings side by side. Stack 1 ring on top, centered over the first 2 rings. Hold the suede lace pieces together as 1 and weave them through the back of the first ring, over the edge of the top ring, under the touching edges of the bottom rings and over the edge of the top ring. The pattern is basically under-over-under-over.

TWO • Continue weaving
Add another bottom ring and another top ring. Weave the suede lace over the edge of the top ring, under the touching edges of the bottom rings and over the edge of the top ring.

THREE • Adjust rings on suede lace
Continue adding rings for a total of 21 rings. Adjust the rings so they're centered on the suede lace.

FOUR • Begin to build central pendant
String a twisted ring and a crystal channel onto a 6mm jump ring and use the jump ring to connect them to the center twisted ring on the necklace.

FIVE • Finish central pendant
Use the 8mm jump ring to connect the 28mm twist pendant to the twisted ring.

SIX • Finish necklace
Holding the suede lace pieces together, place them inside a fold-over crimp. Use chain-nose pliers to fold over each side of the crimp. Repeat for the other end of the necklace. Use a 4mm jump ring to attach half of the clasp to each end of the necklace.

By Fernando DaSilva

Artemis

The centerpiece of this necklace reminds me of the moon, which reminds me of the Greek goddess Artemis. On her third birthday, she requested and got the right to bring light to the world, among other things. She is also associated with forests and nature. Combining the moon symbol with top-drilled opalescent green bicone beads, representing the earth, felt just right. The polyester chain and simple knots in the gray-silver thread add a unique texture.

Materials

1 30mm silver shade twist crystal pendant

6 10mm silver shade Helix crystal beads

30 8mm palace green opal top-drilled crystal bicone pendants

24 6mm palace green opal top-drilled crystal bicone pendants

22 6mm palace green opal crystal rounds

20 wide oval silver-plated tags

1 #6 gray carded silk

12" (31cm) dark green polyester chain

1 6mm silver-plated round jump ring

2 4mm silver-plated round jump ring

1 silver-plated swivel-tie clasp

1 silver-plated pinch bail

Tools

chain-nose pliers

flush cutters

knotter tool

bead stringing glue

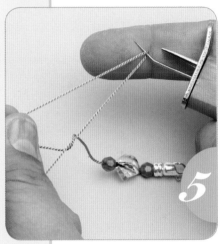

ONE • Pull silk through clasp

Unwrap the silk from its card and stretch it out, holding the ends to get rid of the kinks. Tie an overhand double knot in the silk at the far end from the needle. Pass the silk through the inside bar of half of the swivel clasp, and adjust the tie.

TWO • Knot first bead in place

String 1 round, 1 Helix and 1 round onto the silk, leaving 3" (8cm) of silk at the end. String the thread back through the first round bead strung on and make an overhand knot. Repeat the same step with a Helix bead.

THREE • Apply glue to secure knot

Go back through the last round bead and slide it closer to the last one; apply a dab of bead stringing glue and let it sit, keeping extra silk to be trimmed later.

FOUR • Trim excess silk

Place wire cutters close to the last strung bead and trim away the excess silk.

FIVE • Begin making knot with knotter tool

Insert the awl into the loop away from your hand; remove your fingers and tighten the knot on the awl.

tip

You can use satin silver Bead Bumpers to replace knots on this project. They will keep the beads nicely separated and create a slightly different texture. You can also change up this design by using a different color of polyester chain. It comes in black, brown and gray. Having more options expands your design possibilities.

SIX • Finish knot

Insert silk into the knotter's Y-shaped prong; pull down so that the knot tightens further onto the awl. Pull down on the silk with your free hand. Using the knotter hand and thumb, push up until the knot slides up and off the awl (the knot should be flush against last bead).

SEVEN • String beads onto silk

String beads onto the silk in the following pattern: 3 small pendants, round, 8mm pendant, tag, large pendant, tag, large pendant. Repeat this pattern for a total of 9 large green pendants. String a 9-link piece of polyester chain onto the silk, bringing the thread through the first, fourth and ninth links. String on a Helix bead. At the center of the necklace, reverse the pattern to finish the other half of the necklace. Tie a knot between each green round and each green large crystal pendant only. Once you have finished knotting the strand, string on the last 3 beads in the established pattern and repeat the techniques given in steps 1–4 to finish the necklace.

EIGHT • Create center pendant

Slide the silver shade twist pendant onto a pinch bail and use a crimp tool to secure the pinch bail closed. Link this dangle to a 4mm jump ring. Set it aside. Slide a 9-link piece of polyester chain onto a 6mm jump ring, grabbing the first, fourth and ninth links with the ring. Close it gently. Link the polyester chain dangle to the same jump ring to which the silver shade pendant is linked, holding it from the pendant jump ring so it lays on top of the twist pendant.

NINE • Attach pendant

Link the twisted circle pendant to the center of the necklace with a 4mm jump ring, sliding it between the 2 round beads at the center of the necklace.

Enhance the appeal of your necklace with matching earrings in a quick but unique style. Simply save two equal pieces of the polyester chain and link them to groups of the same color beads as your necklace. Keep the Helix crystal on the bottom to accentuate the rich differences of shapes and textures. Slide on a French wire, insert into your ear, and then admire yourself in the mirror!

Artemis Earrings

By Fernando DaSilva

In Spades

This modern interpretation of classic art deco design feels just right for today's fashions with its timeless black-and-white color combination. Perfect with dressed up summer whites, it is equally happy with shorts and a tee. I have covered the beading wire with black rubber tubing; the alabaster beads lend movement, softening the overall effect. The compliments will come "in spades" when you wear this.

Materials

9 8mm white alabaster diagonal crystal cube beads

6 8mm white alabaster crystal bicones

20" (51cm).018" (.45mm) satin silver 19-strand beading wire

12" (31cm) 1.7mm frost tubing

12" (31cm) 6mm black rubber tubing

1 silver-plated ball magnetic clasp

2 3.5mm oval silver-plated Scrimp findings

5 silver-plated fancy pendant bails

15 silver-plated medium ball-tip head pins

35 1.5mm oval black Bead Bumpers

5 #3 silver-plated crimp beads

12 4mm silver-plated crimp covers

Tools

bead opener

chain-nose pliers

mighty-crimp tool

wire cutters

131

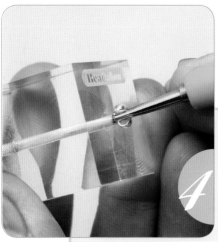

ONE • Cut tubing
Cut 6 ⅞" (2cm) pieces of 6mm black rubber tubing. Cut a 17" (43cm) piece of frost tubing. Cut 2 ⅛" (3mm) pieces and 3 ³⁄₁₆" (5mm) pieces of frost tubing. Set them aside.

TWO • Make dangles
String a black Bead Bumper, 8mm diagonal cube bead, crimp bead, ³⁄₁₆" (5mm) piece of frost tubing and a Bead Bumper onto a ball-tip head pin. Turn a loop above the beads. (See Techniques, page 140, for instructions on turning a loop.) Repeat to make 2 more of these components. String a black Bead Bumper, 8mm diagonal cube, and another Bead Bumper onto a ball-tip head pin. Turn a loop above the beads. Repeat to make a total of 6 dangles. String a black Bead Bumper, 8mm alabaster bicone, #3 crimp bead, ⅛" (3mm) piece of frost tubing, and another Bead Bumper onto a ball-tip head pin. Turn a loop above the beads. Repeat to make a second dangle. String a black Bead Bumper, 8mm alabaster bicone, and another Bead Bumper onto a ball-tip head pin and turn a loop above the beads. Repeat to make a total of 4 dangles. Set all the dangles aside.

THREE • Insert wire into tube
Insert a 20" (51cm) piece of satin silver wire into the 17" (43cm) piece of frost tubing.

FOUR • Open crimp cover
Use a bead opener to widen the crimp covers. This is necessary to ensure that the crimp cover will properly engulf the frost tubing.

FIVE • Close crimp cover over tube
Measure approximately 4" (10cm) from the end of a piece of frost tubing and slide the open crimp cover to that spot. Use the mighty-crimp tool to secure the crimp cover closed over the tubing. (See Techniques, page 138, for instructions on using a crimp cover.)

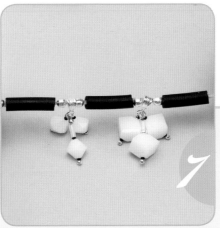

SIX • Slide on first beaded sequence

Slide a ⅞" (2cm) piece of black rubber tubing onto the frost tubing. Flatten another crimp cover in place directly following the black tubing. Attach 1 bicone dangle, 1 bicone-with-tube dangle and a second bicone dangle to the loop of a fancy pendant bail. Squeeze the pinch bail closed and slide the dangles onto the frost tubing. Secure the beaded dangles in place with another crimp cover.

SEVEN • Continue threading on beads and tubes

Slide on another section of black tubing followed by a crimp cover. Slide a diagonal cube dangle, a diagonal-cube-with-tube dangle and another diagonal cube dangle onto the loop of a pinch bail. Squeeze the pinch bail closed and slide the dangles onto the frost tubing. Secure the beaded dangles in place with another crimp cover. Continue threading on dangles on pinch bails alternating with black tubing and securing each section with crimp covers as follows: black tube, diagonal cube dangles, black tube, diagonal cube dangles, black tube, bicone dangles, black tube.

EIGHT • Secure design with Scrimp finding

Loosen the screw in the Scrimp finding, insert the satin wire into the Scrimp finding, through the loop on the magnetic clasp and back through the Scrimp finding. (See Techniques, page 139, for instructions on using a Scrimp finding.) Tighten the screw and cut the excess wire. Make sure to feed as much of the wire as possible through the Scrimp finding until the frost tubing is flush with both Scrimp findings. Tighten the screw and cut the excess wire.

In Spades Earrings

These sassy, swingy earrings make me think of 1930s dancers doing the jitterbug! Slide small pieces of frosted tubing and black tubing onto an eye pin and make a simple loop at the opposite end. Add white crystals to the bottom and then connect each dangle to a triangle-shape ear wire through a white crystal bead link. So much movement, and so full of life!

By Katie Hacker

Skywater

If you've been too intimidated to try a peyote project, then this is the design for you! The peyote bail is a great starter project for learning this bead-weaving technique, and this necklace is an eye-catching way to show off your new skills. If you prefer not to try the peyote bail, then use a jump ring or a simple beaded bail to attach the pendant to the necklace.

Materials

1 30mm silver hammered circle

1 12mm indicolite graphic crystal bead

2 8mm Pacific opal cube crystal beads

64 5mm indicolite crystal bicones

80 4mm Pacific opal crystal rounds

3 gram package of 11/0 matte iris blue cylindrical seed beads

.018" (.45mm) silver-plated 49-strand beading wire

.006" (.15mm) white beading thread

silver elongated cable chain

2-strand sterling silver EZ-Crimp toggle clasp

4 #1 silver crimp beads

4 3mm silver sparkle round metal crimp covers

3 silver ball head pins

adhesive tape or stopper bead

Tools

#12 beading needle

round-nose pliers

chain-nose pliers

mighty-crimp tool or EZ-Crimp pliers

wire cutters

jeweler's cement

Skywater Bracelet

Circle links and indicolite bead links make for a coordinating bracelet that isn't too matchy. The trick to creating jewelry sets with flair is to repeat some of the same design elements, colors and structure.

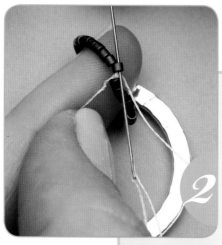

ONE • Make initial beaded loop for peyote bail

Place a piece of tape or a stopper bead 2" (5cm) from the end of a 2-yd (1.8m) length of thread. String 33 seed beads onto the thread. Bring the beaded thread through the hammered circle, then tie the thread ends together to form a loop, linking the beaded loop to the silver circle. Place a drop of jeweler's cement on the knot and remove the tape or stopper bead.

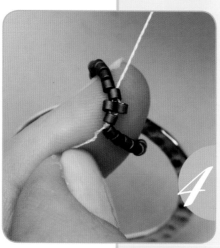

TWO • Begin weaving

Thread a needle onto an end of the thread. Pass the needle through the first bead next to the knot.

THREE • Add first bead

String a bead onto the thread and pass the needle through the third bead.

FOUR • Continue weaving

Continue adding a bead and skipping a bead, adding rows until the bail is the desired width. Weave the end of the thread into the beadwork.

FIVE • String first strand

Cut a 19" (48cm) length of beading wire. Measure 3¼" (8cm) from the end of the wire. Use chain-nose pliers to flatten a crimp bead at that point in the wire. Place a sparkle crimp cover over the flattened crimp bead and use a mighty-crimp tool to close it. String 80 4mm Pacific opal crystal rounds onto the wire. Secure the beads with another crimp bead and sparkle crimp cover.

SIX • Bead second strand

Cut a second 19" (48cm) strand. Secure a crimp bead covered by a crimp cover to the wire, again 3¼" (8cm) from the wire end. String on 64 5mm indicolite crystal bicones and secure the beads as before.

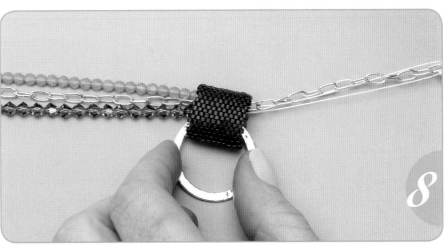

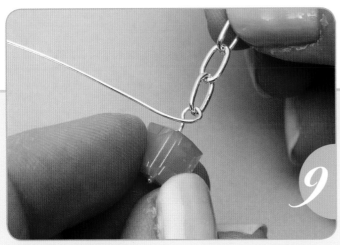

SEVEN • Link beaded strands and chain to clasp

Remove 19" (48cm) of elongated chain. Link an end of the chain to the circle clasp component. Link an end of each beaded strand to the circle clasp component using an EZ-Crimp end. (See Techniques, page 139, for instructions on using EZ-Crimp ends.) Link the free ends of the chain and beaded strands to the bar component of the clasp.

EIGHT • Slide on beaded bail

Hold the beaded wires and the chain together and slide the beaded bail onto the necklace.

NINE • Make dangles

Separate out 3 3-link sections of elongated chain. Slide an 8mm Pacific opal cube crystal bead onto a head pin and turn a loop above the bead. Slide the loop onto the final link in a 3-link chain section and wrap the loop closed. (See Techniques, page 140, for instructions on turning and wrapping a loop.) Make a matching chain-cube dangle and a 12mm indicolite-chain dangle.

TEN • Link dangles to hammered circle

Open the top loop in each chain section and link the chain dangles to the hammered circle.

Techniques

On the following pages, we've collected all the basic techniques used throughout this book for easy reference. Even the most seasoned jewelry makers sometimes have trouble with crimping and looping, so spend time practicing these fundamental methods and check out our tips for improving your techniques. Perfecting these skills will allow you to make jewelry that looks professional and lasts longer.

Using a Crimp Tube or Bead to Attach a Clasp

The most basic way to attach a clasp to beading wire is to use a crimp tube. Crimp tubes are special metal cylinders that provide a secure finish when squeezed closed with a crimping tool. It has recently been discovered that crimping is more successful when the tube is formed into an oval shape before beginning the process of creasing, folding and rounding the tube.

ONE • Pass both wires through crimp bead or tube
Pass a wire end through a crimp bead or tube, through the clasp and back through the crimp.

TWO • Use outer jaw to create oval shape
Place the crimp bead or tube in the outer jaw of the crimping pliers and press down to shape the crimp into an oval.

THREE • Use inner jaw to create indention
Place the crimp bead or tube into the inner jaw and press down to create an indention.

FOUR • Fold crimp bead or tube
Move the crimp bead or tube back to the outer jaw and fold it in half.

FIVE • Cut off wire
Use wire cutters to trim away the excess wire flush with the bottom of the crimp.

SIX • Slide on crimp cover
If you want to cover the crimp tube or bead, slide a crimp cover over it and use the outer jaw of a mighty-crimp tool to squeeze the crimp cover in place.

SEVEN • Covered crimp
When you've squeezed the crimp cover fully closed, the crimp tube or bead will be completely hidden.

Using a Wire Guardian

Wire Guardians provide extra protection where beading wire meets a clasp, much like French wire is used to cover the end of knotted silk jewelry. When used in combination, the Wire Guardian and Scrimp findings provide the most durable connection.

ONE • Thread guardian onto wire
Thread the wire through the Wire Guardian, leaving a short tail.

TWO • Slide clasp onto wire
Thread the clasp onto the wire so it rests in the U-bend of the Wire Guardian. Secure the wires with a crimp bead or tube, or secure them with a Scrimp finding.

Using a Scrimp Finding

These special findings are removable, which allows you to change the clasp or adjust the length of the design after it's finished. The screw holds the beading wire in place inside the finding. To make it permanent, add a drop of Beadfix glue to the screw.

ONE • Slide Scrimp finding onto wires
Slide the Scrimp finding onto both wires, sliding it up the wires so it's approximately ⅛" (3mm) away from the Wire Guardian.

TWO • Screw Scrimp finding in place
Use the screwdriver that comes with the scrimp findings to tighten the Scrimp finding in place.

Using an EZ-Crimp End

An EZ-Crimp end is one of the simplest ways to attach a clasp to beading wire. The coiled center squeezes the wire uniformly, ensuring a secure connection without abrasion of the wire.

ONE • Thread wire into EZ-Crimp end
Thread the end of the wire into the EZ-Crimp end until the end of the wire is flush to the top of the crimp tube portion of the EZ-Crimp end.

TWO • Squeeze EZ-Crimp end to secure wire
Place the EZ-Crimp end in the outer jaws of the mighty-crimp tool and squeeze them to trap the wire inside the tube.

Turning a Loop

Basic loops are a jewelry-making fundamental because they're quick and easy to make. Because they are prone to coming open when pulled, you should only make them with heavy-gauge wire.

ONE • Bend wire at 90 degrees
Slide a bead onto a head pin and use your fingers or round-nose pliers to bend the wire 90 degrees above the bead.

TWO • Use round-nose pliers to make a loop
Grasp the wire just above the bend with round-nose pliers. Use your fingers or a second set of pliers to wrap the wire around 1 of the pincers.

THREE • Cut off excess wire
Use wire cutters to trim the wire directly at the base of the loop.

FOUR • Use chain-nose pliers to close loop
Grasp the loop with chain-nose pliers and use the pincers to make any necessary adjustments to the loop.

Making a Wrapped Loop

Wrapped loops are another essential jewelry-making skill. They're more secure than basic loops because the wrapped portion prevents them from pulling open.

ONE • Bend wire at 90 degrees
Leaving some space above the bead, bend the wire at 90 degrees using your fingers or round-nose pliers. Grasp the wire directly above the bend.

TWO • Loop wire around pliers
Use your fingers or round-nose pliers to wrap the wire around 1 of the pincers.

THREE • Wrap wire around base of loop
Hold the loop with chain-nose pliers and use your fingers or a pair of round-nose pliers to wrap the wire around the base of the loop. Use wire cutters to trim away the wire tail. Use chain-nose pliers to make any fine adjustments to the loop and to tuck in the end of the wire.

140

Opening and Closing a Jump Ring

A jump ring should always be opened by turning one side of the ring as if it's on a hinge. Never pull the ends directly apart.

ONE • Right way
Grasp the jump ring with your fingers on 1 side of the break and with chain- or flat-nose pliers on the other side of the break. Pull the pliers toward you so you're moving the ring laterally.

TWO • Wrong way
Don't open a jump ring this way! Notice how the ends are moving away from each other horizontally and distorting the shape and integrity of the ring.

Tying a Surgeon's Knot

A surgeon's knot is a more secure version of a square knot because it has an extra pass through the last loop. Always add a drop of jeweler's cement to the knot when tying elastic cord.

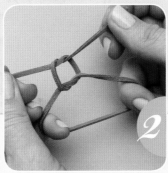

ONE • Make a half knot
Make a half knot, bringing the right strand over the left. (A half knot is the same kind of knot you make when tying your shoe.)

TWO • Make overhand knot
Make another half knot in the opposite direction, bringing the left strand over the right.

THREE • Tighten knot
Bring the end through the loop again, then tighten the knot.

Resources

Most of the supplies you'll need to make the projects in this book can be found at local craft stores and at discount department stores. We've exclusively used beads and components from Beadalon and CRYSTALLIZED - *Swarovski Elements*, but you may substitute anything you feel comfortable working with. Here is a bit of background on the manufacturers of all the supplies, beads and findings featured in this book.

BEADALON
www.beadalon.com

Not all brands of flexible beading wire are equal. For more than thirty years, Beadalon has been the originator, innovator and manufacturer of bead-stringing wire. Beadalon is a family-owned company with a twenty-four-hour production facility in West Chester, Pennsylvania.

Beadalon is unique in the industry because it is the only company that makes its own wire, strand and cable for bead stringing. Other brands simply label and respool wire purchased from third-party factories. The manufacturing difference allows Beadalon to design and produce exciting new wire products in-house, such as the industry's first silver-plated and 24K gold-plated wires. It also enables Beadalon to produce the widest selection of wire flexibilities, diameters, colors and spool lengths.

In addition to beading wire, Beadalon offers a full range of beading supplies, including stringing accessories, cords, findings, organizers, tools and more. Beadalon also creates other innovative products for beading, such as the Scrimp finding, an adjustable, miniature finding with a set screw.

CREATE YOUR STYLE WITH CRYSTALLIZED – *SWAROVSKI ELEMENTS*
www.create-your-style.com

The name Swarovski has been inextricably linked to precision-cut crystal and fashion for more than 113 years. Its trademark highly polished, faceted crystals come in a myriad of shapes, sizes and colors, with new innovations frequently hitting the market.

The company was founded by Daniel Swarovski I, born in 1862 in Northern Bohemia (then the center of a flourishing crystal and costume jewelry industry). He was fascinated with crystal from his earliest years and began the company in 1895 in Wattens, Austria, where he lived near an alpine stream so he could generate his own electricity and keep his inventions safe. His innovative approach to creating precision-cut crystal revolutionized the jewelry and fashion industries and continues to set the standard. Today, the company has grown to 20,000 employees with a presence in more than 120 countries.

Swarovski has worked with iconic figures such as Chanel, Schiaparelli, Balenciaga and later Christian Dior. The light-filled crystals were irresistible to artists such as jazz singer Josephine Baker, and to Hollywood icons including Marlene Dietrich, Marilyn Monroe and Audrey Hepburn. Today, crystal enthusiasts everywhere can create their own unique, personal crystal style with Swarovski's newest line of products for fashion, jewelry and interiors.

CREATE YOUR STYLE focuses on the endless possibilities offered by CRYSTALLIZED – *Swarovski Elements*, the extensive collection of crystal beads, pendants and a myriad of other styles of cut crystal in seemingly endless shapes, sizes, colors and effects. See page 11 for detailed descriptions of different types of CRYSTALLIZED – *Swarovski Elements* beads.

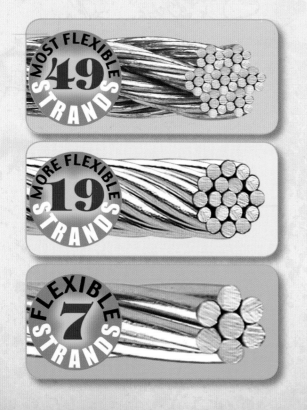

These illustrations show the unique cabled construction of Beadalon wire. The more strands that make up an individual piece of wire, the more flexible the wire.

Index

Find More Great How-To Jewelry Instruction in These North Light Titles

A Charming Exchange
by Kelly Snelling and Ruth Rae

Inside *A Charming Exchange* you'll find the works and words of more than 30 artists with an array of varying creative styles and insights on collaborative art. Learn how to create 25 jewelry projects using a wide variety of techniques, from working with basic jewelry findings, beads and wire to incorporating mixed-media elements such as solder, fabric and found objects into charms and other jewelry projects. The book even offers ideas, inspiration and resources for you to start your own online swaps and collaborations.

ISBN-10: 1-60061-051-X
ISBN-13: 978-160061-051-6
paperback, 128 pages, Z1653

Perfect Match
by Sara Schwittek

Perfect Match is filled to the brim with 40+ fabulous earring designs for all occasions. From a day on the beach to a night out on the town, you will learn how to make earrings to go with every outfit and outing. Sara Schwittek will teach you all about the tools and techniques used to make her fabulous earring designs in as little as 15 minutes. From simple dangles to sophisticated chandeliers, you are sure to find your perfect match!

ISBN-10: 1-60061-068-4
ISBN-13: 978-1-60061-068-4
paperback, 160 pages, Z1803

Beyond the Bead
by Margot Potter

Inside *Beyond the Bead,* you'll find over 20 mixed-media techniques for creating unique beads, pendants and findings from unexpected materials including glass, plastic, clay, hardware store goods, and paper and collage supplies. From molded Buddha heads and glittered locusts to vintage Vogue ladies and etched butterflies, this book is a veritable pu pu platter of crafting ideas.

ISBN-10: 1-60061-105-2
ISBN-13: 978-160061-105-6
paperback, 128 pages, Z2066.

Semiprecious Salvage
by Stephanie Lee

Create clever and creative jewelry that tells a story by combining metal, wire and beads with found objects, some familiar and some unexpected. You'll learn the ins and outs of cold connections, soldering, aging, using plaster, resins and more, all in the spirit of a traveling expedition.

ISBN-10: 1-60061-019-6
ISBN-13: 978-1-60061-019-6
paperback, 128 pages, Z1281

These books and other fine North Light titles are available at your local craft retailer, bookstore or online supplier. Or visit our Web site at www.mycraftivity.com.